Peter Shaffer

Amadeus

edited by
Richard Adams

with a personal essay by
Peter Shaffer

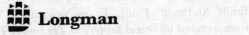
Longman

LONGMAN GROUP UK LIMITED
Longman House
Burnt Mill, Harlow, Essex, CM20 2JE, England
and Associated Companies throughout the world.

This edition © Longman Group Limited 1984
This edition first published by Longman Group Limited
in association with André Deutsch Limited.

ISBN 0 582 35371 8
First published 1984
Third impression 1989

Set in 10/12 pt. Monophoto Baskerville
Produced by Longman Group (FE) Ltd
Printed in Hong Kong

Acknowledgements

We are grateful to the following for permission to reproduce
copyright materials:
André Deutsch for an extract from the preface to *AMADEUS
Version 1* (1980); the author, William Golding for an extract from
a letter to Richard Adams dated 9 Nov 1964; Macmillan London
and Basingstoke for extracts from *Mozart's Letters* translated by
Emily Anderson (1956); Times Newspapers Ltd for an extract
from a review by Brigid Brophy in *The Sunday Times* (4 July 1965).

Contents

A personal essay

by Peter Shaffer

An introduction to three plays: The Royal Hunt of the Sun, Equus and Amadeus

It is hard for me to comment on these plays. I do not much like the idea of an author, as it were, walking along beside his texts, pointing out features of interest in them. As a matter of fact, I do not much like anybody else doing so: as I grow older I confess that I have less and less use for criticism, exegesis, or scholarly essays of explication. In America, where I have spent a fair portion of my time, writing seems to have fallen almost entirely into the hands of commentators.

The pages of this volume contain the material of live theatre. They are of no use to the radio director, the television director, even the cinema director. The material is intended to be brought to physical life in a space which has to be animated afresh each time of playing, by the vibrations of the actors and by those of the spectators. A play, like justice, is pre-eminently a thing *seen* to be done.

This is why, I hope, these three plays possess certain features in common. Each owns a certain flamboyance: a reliance upon gesture to enshrine idea – without which there is no theatre; a desire to enthrall a crowd of watchers – without which there is certainly no theatre; and a strong pleasure in illusion. I imagine that this pleasure has always been a motive with me, ever since as a young boy I laid out a pack of cards on my pillow in bed, and imagined the lives of the Kings, Queens and Jacks rather than play games with them.

It is my object to tell tales; to conjure the spectres of horror and happiness, and fill other heads with the images which have haunted my own. My desire, I suppose, is to perturb and make gasp: to please and make laugh: to surprise. If I am a peacock in this respect, at least I am aware that peacockery is one of the dramatist's obligations. 'Don't show off' is not an adjuration to be made sensibly to playwrights. Needless to say, this does not exonerate in me, or in any writer, excessive spreading of tail-feathers.

The Royal Hunt of the Sun, the earliest of the three, was produced most splendidly by John Dexter and the National Theatre at the Chichester Festival of 1964. Speaking of tail-feathers, I think that this celebrated production used up the entire (and considerable) stock of Chinese pheasant feathers available in England at that time. It was a hugely lavish affair, superbly set and constumed by Michael Annals. The colour supplements of two Sunday newspapers in London devoted astonished articles to its lavishness: this sort of spectacle had not been seen on drab English stages for some while. Audiences responded in tremendous and delighted numbers. To this day I still receive communications from people telling me how they can never forget the opening of the great metal sun near the beginning of the play, or the flood of blood red cloth vomiting out of it later to engulf them in the idea of massacre, or the golden funeral masks of the Incas, with their triangular eyes and copper cheeks, turned yearningly towards the rising sun at the end. This was not lavishness for the sake of it: lavishness was the point. Peru was a kingdom, wrote one mediaeval commentator, where gold was as common as wood in Spain. There was clearly no showing a kingdom of infinite treasures without recourse to some visual splendour. Similarly there was no creating the aural world of sixteenth-century Peru without a strange and continuing music. Many of my plays have used music, but none more elaborately than *The Royal Hunt of the Sun*. In my view Marc Wilkinson's superb score is integral to the play.

Of course I do not mean to imply by any of the above that the words are not important. They are paramount. *The Royal Hunt of the Sun* took me three years to write. So did *Equus*. So did *Amadeus*. I write and destroy the writing; and rewrite, and destroy the rewriting – and I continue in this way until not only the images but the words are entirely clear in my mind, and the flavour of each scene is strong on my tongue. Each play has obviously to acquire a different kind of flavour – the three under discussion here are, after all, set in mediaeval Peru, modern Hampshire, and Enlightenment Vienna respectively; but all are obviously contemporary pieces in the sense that they were written by me and are being read by you.

Equus is obviously less rhetorical than *The Royal Hunt of the Sun*, but many of the same elements appear in it. Again there are masks, only they are now transparent: we see the actor's head through the wire head of the horse – a double image which is the preoccupation of the play. Once again there are raised boots, as in ancient theatre: the Inca in *Royal Hunt* appears before the massacre poised on huge *cothurni*; the horses stalk and stamp round their English stable on high metal hooves. The sound of their feet on the wooden stage, discreetly and alarmingly used, filled the theatre when the play was first produced at the National Theatre in 1973 (again by John Dexter) with an ominous scraping which seemed to herald divine presence. Once more there was music by Marc Wilkinson, this time an eerie humming in twelve tones to recall – in the composer's intention – Vienna, the city of Freud. Perhaps this last was a tenuous connection. All the same the play, as it grew under my hands, came more and more to question the ultimate uses of psychiatry. In the first draft the doctor was drawn more vaguely; less in the central position. In the second draft he grew more prominent, and his self-doubts more important to the meaning of the piece. In London *Equus* caused a sensation because it displayed cruelty to horses; in New York because it allegedly displayed cruelty to psychiatrists.

Of all my plays *Equus* was the most private. I wrote it for myself. I had no notion how popular it was to become – its extraordinary run of well over a thousand performances on Broadway could never have been remotely envisaged by me. The play has been subject to a vast amount of commentary and misuse: a few doctors declaring it a madman's charter; some do-your-own-thingers using it as a means to justify every kind of human aberration. For me it is a deeply erotic play, and also one of tragic conflict. Tragedy obviously does not lie in a conflict of Right and Wrong, but in a collision between two different kinds of Right: in this case, surely, between Dysart's professional obligation to treat a terrified boy who has committed a dreadful crime, and Alan's passionate capacity for worship – his profound desire to cry 'O Magnum Mysterium!' alone in a rubbish-strewn field, his burning ecstasy set against his doctor's careful prosaicism. Dysart has to do what he does. Let no man say 'Do your own thing', for example, to Jack the Ripper. Yet in proceeding by his best and honourable lights, the doctor cannot but know that he is in some clear sense the destroyer of a passion he must forever, and rightly, envy.

Envy, of course, is also the theme of *Amadeus*: Salieri's envy of Mozart's genius. Again I have little to add about this play: what I needed to say on the theme of man's proper objection to divine arbitrariness seems to me to be fairly contained in the work itself. Of course Salieri commits a stupid sin – and I do not mean his persecution of Mozart. He demands a God he can understand. What artist would do that? He says, in effect, 'Let me dip my net into the unfathomable well, and bring up shining creatures hitherto unseen!' But he also says, 'Let me see to the bottom of this well: it is my right as a man! I object to the darkness wherein the connections of beauty are formed.' As well object to the dark of the womb! Confronted by divine mystery, he says merely, 'How dare you?' A fool, you say. And yet he also has his right. (Again the collision of 'Right'.) All he wanted was to serve. To be owned by an Absolute. We need an answer for his torment. True he is condemned to chew forever the cud of his own poisonous sense of fairness – but yet who would dare say that a sense of fairness is dispensable?

Paul Scofield played Salieri at the National Theatre in November 1979, and in New York Ian McKellen played the same part a year later, somewhat rewritten. The reasons for the changes, which were approved by audiences and critics who saw both versions are explained in my preface to the new edition of the play.

Introduction

For the record: the text of Amadeus and other matters

Not long after the publication of his novel *The Spire* in 1964, William Golding was asked by some students to settle a point about his book that had been causing them some difficulties. His reply touches on an important truth about the nature, not only of the novel, but indeed of all creative art:

> I've got past the belief that a man knows what he's written, except in the most general terms – and perhaps not even that. In a word, the book is what you think it is – what you get out of it, rather than what the author thought he put into it.

To put it another way: any work of art – no matter how 'finished' it may seem to be – has an independent life of its own; it changes according to the frame of mind and the circumstances of the reader, watcher or listener. Today, we may see in a play like *The Tempest* things that Shakespeare never intended us to see; we may likewise – because the ways people think and behave have changed enormously over the intervening centuries – miss some of the very points that he most wanted to get across to his audience. But that does not make our response to the play any less valid than that of Shakespeare's contemporaries. Any play – or novel or symphony – grows and changes every time it is experienced afresh.

Peter Shaffer's plays grow and change in another, more obvious sense as well. Nearly all of them have been altered and reshaped by the author after – and very often as a direct result of – their first performances. Shaffer is a firm believer in writing and rewriting until he has established what he wants to say in the clearest and most effective way possible; a firm believer too in getting together with his actors to see what will work best under the lights, on stage, in performance. We are reminded of this by his account in the

Preface to *Amadeus* (see page xxx) of the way in which he revised the scene of the final confrontation between Salieri and Mozart. The result of Shaffer's method of working is that some of his plays – *Amadeus* included – exist in more than one version. *Shrivings* (1974), for example, is a rewriting of an earlier piece called *The Battle of Shrivings*, while *White Liars* (1967) is the final version of a play originally published in America under the title *White Lies*.

Amadeus was premiered in London on 2 November 1979 and the text was published the following year (version 1). On 17 December 1980, the play opened in New York, but in a revised version which – among other things – toned down Mozart's oafish vulgarity and introduced new material to underline the ambivalence of his attitude to his father. This version was published in London and New York in 1981 (version 2). Since then, Peter Shaffer has reworked the text yet again (version 3) and has restored certain details – such as references to Mozart's relationship with his wife's sister, Aloysia – that were originally included in version 1 but dropped from version 2. It is version 3, the most complete and authoritative text of *Amadeus*, that we have used for this edition.

Amadeus, then, is in two important senses a living creation. It has changed its printed shape more than once. In performance, it changes its visual, auditory and emotional shape with each new audience and each change of cast. You will certainly gain much from reading and studying the play, but you will gain infinitely more from going to see a live performance and allowing it to make its impact upon you in the fullest and most direct way possible. *Amadeus* is, after all, as Peter Shaffer says in the personal essay he has written for this edition, something 'to be brought to physical life in a space which has to be animated afresh each time of playing, by the vibrations of the actors and by those of the spectators' (see page vi). But wherever and however you experience this play, remember that it is *your* reaction to it that matters and that gives it meaning. The author cannot interpret it for you, and it is certainly not the aim of the introduction and notes in this edition to tell you what to think – rather to help free

you, to encourage you to do the thinking and responding for
yourself.

The origins of Amadeus

It was very shortly after the death of Wolfgang Amadeus Mozart
at one in the morning of 5 December 1791 that rumours started to
go about to the effect that his fellow composer and rival, Antonio
Salieri, had poisoned him. Just before Salieri's abortive suicide
attempt in November 1823, the now demented old man is said to
have revived and confirmed these rumours. Seven years later, the
Russian writer Alexander Pushkin wrote a short verse drama
about the poisoning entitled *Mozart and Salieri* (first performed in
1832, and turned into an opera in 1898 by another Russian,
Rimsky-Korsakov). Most serious Mozart scholars today discount
the poisoning theory: it is the stuff of folklore, not of history. In
Amadeus, Peter Shaffer shows Salieri administering not a literal
poison but a figurative one.

Shaffer's sources must certainly have included Pushkin's 'little
tragedy', however. A number of narrative details have found their
way into *Amadeus* unmodified: Salieri's burning ambition to
achieve greatness as a composer, for instance; his envy of the
careless ease with which Mozart can write music of unarguable
genius; finally, his decision – while pretending to be the younger
man's friend – to engineer his destruction.

For other material, Shaffer has turned to the known facts of
Mozart's life and from them has constructed a more or less
accurate account of the events of the composer's last ten years.
Sometimes the merest hints in the documentary records are the
seeds from which grow full-blown scenes: authority for the hanky-
panky at one of Baroness Waldstädten's parties (pages 36–37), for
example, is found in a letter dated 29 April 1782 in which Mozart
takes his wife-to-be to task for allowing a *chapeau* (gentleman) to
measure her calves during a game of forfeits. Certain well-known
and oft-repeated Mozart anecdotes are also woven into the play's

fabric: the composer's waspish retort when Joseph II had the temerity to suggest that *Die Entführung aus dem Serail* had 'too many notes' (page 30) or the famous account of the six-year-old Mozart's 'proposal' to Marie Antoinette at Schönbrunn (page 23). Mozart's letters also provide ample evidence of the strain which for many years existed in his relationship with his father, Leopold, and Shaffer makes this an important and recurring theme in his play. We are constantly reminded of Leopold's reluctance to give his blessing to his son's marriage to Constanze Weber and of the manner in which he attempted to exercise a dour paternal control even from Salzburg.

Only comparatively rerely does Shaffer bend the record slightly in order to create a particular dramatic effect, as when he suggests that it was Mozart who made the running in his relationship with Josephine Aurnhammer, rather than the other way about. He clearly does so because the notion of her husband's promiscuity provides suitable ammunition for Constanze to hurl at Mozart during one of their periodic rows (pages 38–39). *Amadeus* does not, after all, set out to be a minutely accurate factual record. Its truth is not that of the history book, but of the theatre. The playwright who draws his material from historical sources must always be free to include or omit, to exaggerate or diminish, to alter the balance of fact in whatever way is necessary for him to establish the *dramatic* truth that he is seeking.

Mozart's language

One of the dramatic truths that Peter Shaffer brings out in *Amadeus* is that it is possible for a man of great genius, a creator of sublime beauty, to be at the same time an unattractive, even vulgar figure. To do this he makes his character speak in an exaggerated version of the style the real-life Mozart occasionally adopted in letters he wrote to his cousin Maria Anna Thekla Mozart (known affectionately as 'Bäsle'). The chief features of this style were a tendency to lapse into nonsense rhyming and frequent reference to bowel functions. Here is the opening of a letter dated 5 November 1777:

> Dearest Coz Fuzz!
> I have received reprieved your dear letter, telling selling me that my uncle carbuncle, my aunt can't and you too are very well hell. Thank God, we too are in excellent health wealth. Today the letter setter from my Papa Ha! Ha! dropped safely into my claws paws ...

In another, dated 28 February 1778, Mozart apologizes for not having written to Bäsle and asks

> ... whether to make peace with me you'll be so kind? If not, I'll swear I'll let off one behind! Ah, you're laughing! Victoria! Our arses shall be the symbol of our peacemaking ...

And so on. The fact Shaffer uses these occasional lapses into childish crudity as the foundation for Mozart's stage personality and vocabulary caused a certain amount of protest when *Amadeus* was first performed. Some people are still unable to accept his characterization. Their resistance suggests that they do not appreciate that in the theatre the dead-and-gone historical Mozart is of no account, that their interest and attention should be focused entirely on the character who comes to bounding life before them in the spotlight.

Mozart and Vienna

The Vienna of *Amadeus* is a far from satisfactory place. Capital of a sprawling empire, temple of culture, centre of the musical world, it is at the same time riddled with hypocrisy and self-interest. It is ruled by an emperor whose tastes in music, though boyishly enthusiastic, are decidedly superficial, whose court and *kapelle* (with the single and ironic exception of Salieri himself) are entirely incapable of recognizing true genius – a shortcoming shared by the citizens of Vienna at large. The city is rife with gossip, Salieri's venticelli being scarcely able to suppress the excitement with which they pass on the latest tattle. The pervading veneer of sophistication is paper-thin and all too easily peeled away. The court vogue for speaking in any civilized language but one's own (the gush of French and Italian in the scene of Mozart's first meeting with the emperor, the coining of such absurd hybrids as 'Caro Herr') degenerates into the deliberate setting up of language barriers. It is with some justification that Strack complains of the excess of Italian 'chittero-chattero' when he is excluded from the plottings of Salieri and Rosenberg over *Le Nozze di Figaro*. Cosmopolitanism turns all too rapidly into chauvinism as anti-Italian, anti-German, anti-French sentiments are, in their turn, expressed according to the demands of rancour or pettymindedness.

It is into this world of teetering affectation and thinly-veiled malice that Mozart erupts, with his absurd wig and his whinnying giggle. 'Shit-talking Mozart' he may be to the outraged Salieri, but he is also a fresh breeze blowing through the rarified atmosphere of the salons and opera houses. Though he can match the pseudo-sophisticated foreign talk of the courtiers, he is more obviously at home with the nursery games and the homely Austrianisms he shares with his 'botty-smacking wife'. He is a straight talker: forthright in his attitudes, downright in his opinions, careless over aggravating others, oblivious of the offence he causes – unlike Salieri or Strack or van Swieten with their discreet reserve. Without denying or compromising his own individuality he does not, of course, stand a chance of overcoming the prejudice and philistinism of those who patronize and pretend to befriend him. But the thought does not even enter his head; he remains naïvely and refreshingly himself. His declaration of his own genius is, as far as he is concerned, nothing other than a plain statement of fact. With him there is no more room for false modesty than there is for any other kind of hypocrisy. Delicacy, politeness, tact are adult concepts entirely alien to him. He remains an innocent, a child in the fullest – though not always the best – sense of the word. Salieri sees Mozart's honest humanity as nothing short of bestial; he stigmatizes him with his natural appetites and attitudes as the Creature. He works – as the play unfolds to show us – to undermine and destroy the Creature in a typically covert, courtly, Viennese way.

Mozart's clash with the so-called enlightened society of his day raises some important issues. He cannot, after all, help being either who or what he is: unvarnished son of a small-town *kapellmeister* – yes – but also (to use Salieri's words) 'a voice of God', the Magic Flute through whom is breathed a music so sublime that it cannot fail to survive in a world where most else must inevitably pass away. He cannot be the one without being the other – but that does not stop society demanding that he should. Are our expectations of men and women in the public eye significantly different today? Do we require our great creative artists, performers, thinkers to conform to some artificial code of behaviour, embracing such standards as – say – doing a 'proper' day's work, being 'normally' sexually orientated, avoiding 'undesirable' habits? Or are we more enlightened than the men and women of Shaffer's Enlightenment? Is it not perhaps the case that a part of true genius lies in nonconformity?

Why Mozart?

The novelist Brigid Brophy once described Mozart as

the artist whose creative imagination and intelligence are perhaps the best vindication the human species could push forward, were the evolutionary process to ask why humanity should not be scrapped and replaced.

This is a view shared by a remarkably large number of people; but it is not one to which we *have* to subscribe before we can make head or tail of Shaffer's play. We do not even need to know much about

Mozart's music in order to understand what the author is getting at. *Amadeus* does not stand or fall according to whether or not we find the finale of *Figaro* unbearably moving or the starling song from the seventeenth piano concerto teasingly unforgettable. The music does not, in one sense, matter a great deal. Even in the theatre we hear only brief fragments, and these are filtered to our ears through Salieri's fevered consciousness. If our experience of the play is to be limited to reading it alone or with a group of friends, then all we have to keep us in touch with the sound of Mozart is a sequence of printed references.

What matters much more than our opinion of Mozart or familiarity with his music is that we should be capable of understanding what it is like to be Salieri: to know that it is *possible* to be challenged, excited, overwhelmed – in the end, humiliated – by what another human being has created; to be able to share something of the torment and the awe he feels at the moment of his first encounter with the 'Absolute Beauty' that he knows must cause all his achievements to pale into insignificance. If it helps our understanding we can even replace Mozart's music with some other achievement or object that excites our envy and admiration. We all have our own notions of perfection.

The importance of the operas

Being able to cope with the broad issues of *Amadeus* without having 'discovered' Mozart for ourselves is one thing, but appreciating the skill with which Peter Shaffer weaves together elements from the composer's life and his operas without a certain amount of specialist knowledge is very much another. It is only when we know something of the power of the miraculous flute in *Die Zauberflöte*, for example, that we can fully understand what Salieri is getting at when he refers to Mozart as God's Magic Flute, the instrument through which He makes His voice heard on earth. The two heroines of the opera *Così fan Tutte* become associated with the two great loves of Mozart's life, the sisters Aloysia and

Constanze Weber. In a similar way, the harsh accusing figure of the Commendatore in *Don Giovanni* and the benign forgiving one of Sarastro in *Die Zauberflöte* become stage projections of the composer's ambivalent attitude to a father whom at one moment he hates and fears, at another loves and respects.

There are occasions in *Amadeus* when Shaffer makes even more detailed operatic cross-references, using appropriate musical quotations to underpin the action on the stage. In the scene of his first presentation at court (page 27), for instance, Mozart turns Salieri's trite little march of welcome into the tune that operagoers since 1786 have known as the aria 'Non più andrai' from *Le Nozze di Figaro*. In the opera, this aria is used by Figaro to warn the page Cherubino that he must now forget the pleasures and advantages of the past and look forward to a life of hardships. The playing of the theme at the precise moment in *Amadeus* when Salieri's life is about to be dramatically changed by the younger composer's arrival in Vienna is, of course, splendidly ironical. And the fact that it is Mozart who plays the music only serves to intensify the irony. A similar dramatic point is made by the quotation of the melody of the terzetto 'Soave sia il vento' from *Così fan Tutte* just after Salieri's reference to his own work becoming 'calmed in convention' (page 73).

These and other examples of Shaffer's skill in using Mozart's music to emphasize particular themes and twists in the plot of *Amadeus* are examined in detail in the notes to this edition.

Shaffer and music

All of which cannot fail to draw our attention to the fact that Peter Shaffer clearly knows a good deal about his subject. Music has indeed always played an important part in his life. For a while he worked for the London music publishers, Boosey and Hawkes, and in 1961–62 he contributed regular concert reviews to the magazine *Time and Tide*. Not surprisingly, his plays contain a wide range of musical reference. In *Black Comedy* (1965) there is a street named after Scarlatti and an electricity board employee called Schuppanzigh (the original Schuppanzigh was an eighteenth-century violinist and friend of Beethoven). The very title of an earlier play, *Five Finger Exercise* (1958), suggests the way in which, like a pianist loosening up before a performance, its characters flex themselves, without however producing any real warmth or harmony. *The Private Ear* (1962) actually calls for two long sequences of recorded music, the second of which – the love-duet from Puccini's opera *Madam Butterfly* – lasts a full six minutes uninterrupted by dialogue. The soaring passion of the music is intended to contrast starkly with the fumbling inadequacy of the bedsit lovers on stage.

Two of Shaffer's plays use music specially composed to supply the effects he wants to achieve: the Spanish organ music and the Inca chants and bells are as much part of the 'spectacle' of *The Royal Hunt of the Sun* (1964) as its lavish visual effects; in *Equus* (1973) the eerie twelve-note humming serves to build up both a tension and a sense of mystery.

The music of Amadeus

Amadeus depends for its stage effect – more than any of its predecessors – on a number of precise and carefully integrated musical quotations. These quotations are designed to act as landmarks in the last ten years of Mozart's life and career and also to convey something of the composer's genius as it is perceived by his great rival. We should note, however, that it is not Shaffer's intention that the music be presented to the audience 'straight'. In his preface to version 1 of *Amadeus*, he acknowledges the work of Harrison Birtwistle in preparing the score:

Mr Birtwistle is a distinguished composer in his own right, who brilliantly solved the problem of how Mozart's music should sound as heard by Salieri. It was never cheaply distorted by modern devices, yet its subtle 'treatment' suggested the sublime

work of a genius being experienced by another musician's
increasingly agonized mind.

The Mozart quotations – important as they are – are however
by no means the only music in *Amadeus*. The play contains a good
deal of in-built verbal music, heard both in the interplay of voices
in particular scenes and also in some of Salieri's longer set-piece
speeches. The most outstanding example of the former occurs in
the very first scene, which Shaffer directs should have 'the air of a
fast and dreadful Overture'. At first, as the auditorium lights dim,
all we can hear is a hissing whisper, coming to us from all parts of
the theatre. Gradually, two identifiable sounds emerge from this
background, the words 'Salieri' and 'assassin'. As the lights
brighten on the stage, so the intensity of the whispering increases
and we are able to see that it comes principally from the citizens of
Vienna, grouped in silhouette at the back of the acting area. Their
whispering continues – now rising, now subsiding – for the entire
duration of the scene. The venticelli hurry on to the stage, one
from either side. Their voices are like those of two carefully
matched musical instruments, playing their gossipy tunes against
the citizens' more sinister accompaniment. As in a piece of
orchestral music, the two 'instruments' echo or half-echo each
other's motifs; they complement each other, the one finishing a
line begun by the other; they join together and, for special
emphasis, play certain snatches of their music in unison. The
effectiveness of this verbal music can only be fully appreciated in
live performance, but Shaffer gives plenty of clues in the printed
text as to what he has in mind. Notice, for example, the sense of
urgency he builds in the first half of the scene, up to the moment of
Salieri's great cry of 'MOZART!!!' (pages 1–3). The text is
carefully laid out in sections, short at first, but gradually
increasing in length. The climax of each of the first four of these
sections is the word 'Salieri!' But notice how Shaffer indicates the
deepening intensity he wants the actors to convey in their
whispering by having the word printed first in *italic*, then in
Roman capitals. The whole scene certainly repays this sort of close

analysis. But an even more effective way to come to an understanding and enjoyment of its music is to rehearse and read it in a group of about a dozen people. This requires careful thought and preparation. You should, for instance, ensure that the principal voices are suitably contrasted. You should watch out for the many moments where emphasis is subtly varied in adjoining lines or where there are dramatic changes in volume – from *fortissimo* outburst to silence and near silence.

The other kind of verbal music – that to be found in some of the play's longer speeches – is also evident in other works by Shaffer: *Shrivings* and *Equus* both contain outstanding examples. The fact is that, like Bernard Shaw before him, Shaffer possesses an ear sensitive to the natural musical qualities of the English language. His choice of the right-sounding, as well as the right-meaning, word for the context; his ability to balance phrases, to modulate sentences so that they have a clear sense of rise and fall; his control of pace, tone and rhythm – all these features of his style bring to his speeches something of the character of operatic arias. Consider Salieri's great address to his God at the end of Act I. Ideally, of course, you should hear such a piece performed in the theatre by an actor familiar with the role. But failing that, you might try reading it aloud for yourself. Like Shaw, Shaffer gives plenty of indication on the printed page as to how he wants his music to be played. Notice the way in which this entire speech builds to a climax, how the speed and volume of his words increase as Salieri's passion grows. Notice the violence suggested by certain repetitions and near-repetitions, the bitter irony of the interjections in Italian:

> *Capisco!* I know my fate. Now for the first time I feel my emptiness as Adam felt his nakedness ... (*Slowly he rises to his feet.*) Tonight at an inn somewhere in this city stands a giggling child who can put on paper, without actually setting down his billiard cue, casual notes which turn my most considered ones into lifeless scratches. *Grazie*, Signore! You gave me the desire to serve you – which most men do not have – then saw to it the

service was shameful in the ears of the server. *Grazie!* You gave me the desire to praise you – which most do not feel – then made me mute. *Grazie tanti!* You put into me perception of the Incomparable – which most men never know! – then ensured that I would know myself forever mediocre. (*His voice gains power.*) *Why? . . . What is my fault?* . . . Until this day I have pursued virtue with rigour. I have laboured long hours to relieve my fellow men. I have worked and worked the talent you allowed me.(*Calling up*) *You know how hard I've worked!* – solely that in the end, in the practice of the art which alone makes the world comprehensible to me, I might hear Your Voice! And now I do hear it – and it says only one name: MOZART! . . . Spiteful, sniggering, conceited, infantine Mozart! – who has never worked one minute to help another man! – shit-talking Mozart with his botty-smacking wife! – *him* you have chosen to be your sole conduct! And *my* only reward – my sublime privilege – is to be the sole man alive in this time who shall clearly recognize your Incarnation! (*Savagely*) *Grazie e grazie ancora!* (*Pause*) So be it! From this time we are enemies, You and I! I'll not accept it from You – *Do you hear?* . . . They say God is not mocked. I tell you, *Man* is not mocked! . . . *I* am not mocked! . . . They say the spirit bloweth where it listeth: I tell you NO! It must list to virtue or not blow at all! (*Yelling*) *Dio Ingiusto!* – You are the Enemy! I name Thee now – *Nemico Eterno!* And this I swear. To my last breath I shall *block* you on earth, as far as I am able!

This is certainly not a naturalistic speech, but it is nothing if not musical. And yet one of the great ironies of *Amadeus* lies in the fact that Shaffer gives such richly passionate (though disturbed) melodies *not* to Mozart, but to Salieri, the self-acknowledged musical mediocrity. For the man who within a cage of meticulous ink strokes can capture 'an Absolute Beauty', he supplies little more than awkward, coarse-tongued banalities. But, as we have already seen, he has particular reasons for doing so.

The tone of Amadeus

Salieri is without question the central figure in *Amadeus*. He is both narrator and protagonist; he is also the lens through which we view the major issues of the play. Yet the play is named not after him but after the innocent adversary with whose destruction he becomes so grindingly obsessed. 'Amadeus' means 'the man whom God loves'. But it is a strange love that denies Mozart the recognition he deserves, that allows him to be worn to death by poverty and ill health, while according fame and comfort to a man who knows full well that he has no claim to them. These are just two of the many ironies (and we have already noticed several others in passing) that characterize Shaffer's play and give it its special flavour.

Amadeus combines the elements of both comedy and tragedy. On the one hand, it takes us out of ourselves with its wittily inventive dialogue and visual effects; on the other, it focuses our attention on the dark uncertainties of human existence. There is something of the heroic in Salieri's struggle against an inscrutable destiny. The challenge he hurls at his *Dio Ingiusto* in his great Act I speech would do credit to King Lear. But unlike the tragic heroes of Shakespeare or Sophocles, he can escape from the furnace of his suffering and view the entire experience with comic detachment:

'What use, after all, is Man, if not to teach God His lessons?' In spite of the various reverses his plans receive in the course of the play, Salieri never really learns the lesson that he cannot supplant destiny in the ordering of his affairs. The greatest irony – and the most tragi-comic of all – lies in his abortive suicide attempt. Even in the matter of cutting his own throat he remains a mediocrity.

Amadeus is calculated to make us think: it deals with important issues in a sensitive and intelligent manner. I have tried to identify some of these in the course of this introduction. But it is also a skilfully-crafted entertainment, designed to divert and enthrall the theatre audience. It is because it combines these two vital qualities that it has played to packed houses on both sides of the Atlantic, has already been translated into a number of foreign languages and has been adapted for the cinema. There seems little doubt that it will hold its place in the theatre for many years to come.

Preface

Amadeus opened at the National Theatre of Great Britain in November 1979. According to Peter Hall, the director of the play and of the theatre, it constituted the single greatest success enjoyed by this celebrated institution since its founding. At the moment of writing, one year after its premiere, the *Sunday Times* of London reports that audiences begin lining up at six o'clock in the morning to buy the few tickets which are sold only on the day of performance. This is hardly a usual practice with the Great British Public.

I mention these agreeable facts only so that I may be believed when I assert that it is not because the play was a failure in England that I made changes when it came to be produced in America. On the contrary, it is entirely the exciting success of the piece which has emboldened me to try to improve it.

The entire run of *Amadeus* in Washington, where the play was presented prior to its appearance at the Broadhurst Theatre in New York, was characterized by the most intense work. I have never before altered material in a play so extensively. I was led on to do this by what became a nearly obsessive pursuit of clarity, structural order, and drama. I was supported in these endeavours by the most understanding of directors, as well as by the most enthusiastic company of actors and the most patient stage management. I would like to thank them all deeply for their unflagging help – without which, truly, this work could not possibly have been achieved.

One of the faults which I believe existed in the London version was simply that Salieri had too little to do with Mozart's ruin. In the second act he was too often reduced to prowling hungrily around the outside of the composer's apartment, watching his decline without sufficiently contributing to it. Dramatically speaking, Salieri seemed to me to be too much the observer of the calamities he should have been causing. Now, in this new version, he seems to me to stand where he properly belongs – at the wicked centre of the action.

This new, more active Salieri offers himself as a substitute father when Leopold Mozart dies. He establishes a much closer human contact with Wolfgang. And he finally induces the trusting composer to betray the rituals of the Freemasons in *The Magic Flute*. I have of course taken certain liberties with this part of the story. I have no reason to believe that the Masons actually repudiated Mozart, or that Baron Van Swieten announced that he would never speak to him again. Nevertheless, Masonic anger over *The Magic Flute* constitutes one of the most persistent rumours attached to the Mozartian legend; and the worthy Baron actually did pay for a third-class funeral, when he could have easily afforded much better for the composer he had patronized, which does suggest some deep offence which Mozart had given him. Indeed, one totally absurd story, which never quite dies out, actually implicates the Masons in causing Mozart's early death!

The great gain in dramatic terms is that I can now show the (factually true) visit of Salieri and his mistress to a performance of *The Magic Flute*. I must confess to a fondness for this new scene. It is rowdy and vigorous; it contains devices of mime which are pleasingly theatrical; it dramatizes the moment – previously only hinted at – when Salieri perceives Mozart to be himself the flute of God; and it enables me to transform the huge accusing silhouette of Leopold-as-Commendatore, seen on the backdrop, into the forgiving silhouette of Leopold-as-Sarastro, his hands extended to the world in a vast embrace of love. This transformation immeasurably clarifies the mental journey which Mozart made from *Don Giovanni* to *The Magic Flute* . . .

The main change in *Amadeus*, however, is concerned with the treatment of the Masked Figure who came to Mozart to commission a Requiem Mass, and whom Mozart in the frenzy of his sick imagination came to regard as the Messenger of Death.

In London this figure was actually Salieri's grim servant Greybig, a religious fanatic dispatched by his murderous master to drive Mozart towards madness. My dissatisfaction with this theatrical idea lay mainly in my awareness that Salieri could not possibly guess that Mozart would react to the appearance of the Figure in the demented way we know he did. This was to read history backwards. And anyway, such tactics did not consort at all with the character of my oblique and indirect villain. My unease ended in the total removal of Greybig from the play, since he had no other real function than to be this Messenger of Death.

There ensued what was for me a tense period in Washington, after we had already opened the play, when I experimented with a series of new confrontation scenes between Salieri and Mozart, dispensing with a masked figure altogether. Ian McKellen and Tim Curry – the actors chiefly concerned – were heroic in assisting me – putting in, playing, and taking out several versions of this climactic passage. Their patience and dedication finally enabled me to discover what I wanted. The play now boasts a much better scene on a human level than the one we played in London. I even finally replaced the mask on Salieri's face: but by this time he was not a crudely melodramatic figure – a spooky, improbable Messenger of Death – but a more poetic and dangerous apparition, a Messenger of God stepping out of Mozart's confessed dreams. This scene was composed with the active and generous encouragement of Peter Hall, who displayed throughout this period of trial a most miraculous calm, and who staged the final version with superb assurance. The unmasking of Salieri by Mozart from behind, for example, is a wonderful gestural climax which relieved the scene of any coarseness. No praise can be too high for Hall's creative skill under pressure . . .

Peter Shaffer

The set

Amadeus can and should be played in a variety of settings. What is described in this text is to a large extent based on the exquisite formulation found for the play by the designer John Bury, helped into being by the director, Peter Hall. I was of course in enthusiastic agreement with this formulation, and set it down here as a tribute to exquisite work.

The set consisted basically of a handsome rectangle of patterned wood, its longest sides leading away from the viewer, set into a stage of ice-blue plastic. This surface shifted beguilingly under various lights played upon it, to show gunmetal grey, or azure, or emerald green, and reflected the actors standing upon it. The entire design was undeniably modern, yet it suggested without self-consciousness the age of the Rococo. Costumes and objects were sumptuously of the period, and should always be so wherever the play is produced.

The rectangle largely represented interiors: especially those of Salieri's salon; Mozart's last apartment; assorted reception rooms, and opera houses. At the back stood a grand proscenium sporting gilded cherubs blowing huge trumpets, and supporting grand curtains of sky-blue, which could rise and part to reveal an enclosed space almost the width of the area downstage. Into this space superb backdrops were flown, and superb projections thrown, to show the scarlet boxes of theatres, or a vast wall of gold mirrors with an immense golden fireplace, representing the encrusted Palace of Schönbrunn. In it also appeared silhouettes of scandal-mongering citizens of Vienna, or the formal figures of the Emperor Joseph II of Austria and his brocaded courtiers. This wonderful upstage space, which was in effect an immense Rococo peep show, will be referred to throughout this text as the Light Box.

*   *   *   *

On stage, before the lights are lowered in the theatre, four objects are to be seen by the audience. To the left, on the wooden rectangle, stands a small table, bearing a cake-stand. In the centre, further upstage and also on the wood, stands a wheelchair of the eighteenth century, with its back to us. To the right, on the reflecting plastic, stands a beautiful fortepiano in a marquetry case. Above the stage is suspended a large chandelier showing many globes of opaque glass.

All directions will be given from the viewpoint of the audience.

Changes of time and place are indicated throughout by changes of light.

In reading the text it must be remembered that the action is wholly continuous. Its fluidity is ensured by the use of servants played by actors in eighteenth-century livery, whose role it is to move the furniture and carry on props with ease and correctness, while the action proceeds around them. Through a pleasant paradox of theatre their constant coming and going, bearing tables, chairs or cloaks, should render them virtually invisible, and certainly unremarkable. This will aid the play to be acted throughout in its proper manner; with the sprung line, gracefulness and energy for which Mozart is so especially celebrated.

*　　*　　*　　*

The asterisks which now and then divide the page indicate changes of scene: but there is to be no interruption. The scenes must flow into one another without pause from the beginning to the end of the play.

CHARACTERS

ANTONIO SALIERI
WOLFGANG AMADEUS MOZART
CONSTANZE WEBER, wife to Mozart
JOSEPH II, Emperor of Austria
COUNT JOHANN KILIAN VON STRACK, groom of the Imperial Chamber
COUNT FRANZ ORSINI-ROSENBERG, Director of the Imperial Opera
BARON GOTTFRIED VAN SWIETEN, Prefect of the Imperial Library
TWO 'VENTICELLI', 'Little Winds': purveyors of information, gossip and rumour
MAJOR DOMO
SALIERI'S VALET   (silent part)
SALIERI'S COOK   (silent part)
TERESA SALIERI, wife of Salieri   (silent part)
KATHERINA CAVALIERI, Salieri's pupil   (silent part)
CITIZENS OF VIENNA

The VENTICELLI also play the TWO GALLANTS at the party in Act One.

The CITIZENS OF VIENNA also play the SERVANTS who move furniture and bring on props as required, and TERESA SALIERI and KATHERINA CAVALIERI, neither of whom have any lines to speak.

The action of the play takes place in Vienna in November 1823, and in recall, the decade 1781–1791.

Act One

Vienna

Darkness.

Savage whispers fill the theatre. We can distinguish nothing at first from this snake-like hissing save the word Salieri! *repeated here, there and everywhere around the theatre.*

Also, the barely distinguishable word Assassin!

The whispers overlap and increase in volume, slashing the air with wicked intensity. Then the light grows upstage to reveal the silhouettes of men and women dressed in the top hats and skirts of early nineteenth century – Citizens of Vienna, all crowded together in the Light Box, and uttering their scandal.

WHISPERERS   *Salieri! . . . Salieri! . . . Salieri!*

Downstage in the wheelchair with his back to us, sits an old man. We can just see, as the light grows a little brighter, the top of his head encased in an old cap, and perhaps the shawl wrapped around his shoulders.

     Salieri! . . . Salieri! . . . Salieri!

Two middle-aged gentlemen hurry in from either side, also wearing the long cloaks and tall hats of the period. These are the Two Venticelli: purveyors of fact, rumour and gossip throughout the play. They speak rapidly – in this first appearance extremely rapidly – so that the scene has the air of a fast and dreadful Overture. Sometimes they speak to each other; sometimes to us – but always with the urgency of men who have ever been first with the news.

VENTICELLO 1   I don't believe it.
VENTICELLO 2   I don't believe it.
VENTICELLO 1   I don't believe it.
VENTICELLO 2   I don't believe it.
WHISPERERS   *Salieri!*

VENTICELLO 1   They say.
VENTICELLO 2   I hear.

1

VENTICELLO 1	I hear.
VENTICELLO 2	They say.
VENTICELLO 1 and VENTICELLO 2	*I don't believe it!*
WHISPERERS	*Salieri!*

VENTICELLO 1	The whole City is talking.
VENTICELLO 2	You hear it all over.
VENTICELLO 1	The cafés.
VENTICELLO 2	The Opera.
VENTICELLO 1	The Prater.
VENTICELLO 2	The gutter.
VENTICELLO 1	They say even Metternich repeats it.
VENTICELLO 2	They say even Beethoven, his old pupil.
VENTICELLO 1	But why now?
VENTICELLO 2	After so long?
VENTICELLO 1	Thirty-two years!
VENTICELLO 1 and VENTICELLO 2	*I don't believe it!*
WHISPERERS	SALIERI!

VENTICELLO 1	They say he shouts it out all day!
VENTICELLO 2	I hear he cries it out all night!
VENTICELLO 1	Stays in his apartments.
VENTICELLO 2	Never goes out.
VENTICELLO 1	Not for a year now.
VENTICELLO 2	Longer. Longer.
VENTICELLO 1	Must be seventy.
VENTICELLO 2	Older. Older.
VENTICELLO 1	Antonio Salieri –
VENTICELLO 2	The famous musician –
VENTICELLO 1	Shouting it aloud!
VENTICELLO 2	Crying it aloud!
VENTICELLO 1	Impossible.
VENTICELLO 2	Incredible.
VENTICELLO 1	I don't believe it!
VENTICELLO 2	I don't believe it!
WHISPERERS	SALIERI!

VENTICELLO 1   I know who *started* the tale!
VENTICELLO 2   *I* know who started the tale!

Two old men – one thin and dry, one very fat – walk onstage, from either side : Salieri's Valet and Pastry Cook.

VENTICELLO 1   (*indicating him*) The old man's valet!
VENTICELLO 2   (*indicating him*) The old man's cook!
VENTICELLO 1   The Valet hears him shouting!
VENTICELLO 2   The Cook hears him crying!
VENTICELLO 1   What a story!
VENTICELLO 2   What a scandal!

The Venticelli move quickly upstage, one on either side, and each collects a silent informant.
Venticello 1 walks down eagerly with the Valet; Venticello 2 walks down eagerly with the Cook.

VENTICELLO 1   (*to Valet*) What does he say, your Master?
VENTICELLO 2   (*to Cook*) What does he cry, the Kapellmeister?
VENTICELLO 1   Alone in his house –
VENTICELLO 2   All day and all night –
VENTICELLO 1   What sins does he shout?
VENTICELLO 2   The old fellow –
VENTICELLO 1   The recluse –
VENTICELLO 2   What horrors have you heard?
VENTICELLO 1 and VENTICELLO 2   *Tell us! Tell us! Tell us at once! What does he cry? What does he cry? What does he cry?*

Valet and Cook gesture towards Salieri.

SALIERI   (*in a great cry*) MOZART!!!

Silence.

VENTICELLO 1   (*whispering*) Mozart!
VENTICELLO 2   (*whispering*) Mozart!
SALIERI   *Perdonami, Mozart! Il tuo assassino ti chiede perdono!*
VENTICELLO 1   (*in disbelief*) Pardon, Mozart!
VENTICELLO 2   (*in disbelief*) Pardon your assassin!

3

VENTICELLO 1 and VENTICELLO 2   *God preserve us!*
SALIERI   *Pietà, Mozart. Mozart pietà!*
VENTICELLO 1   Mercy, Mozart!
VENTICELLO 2   Mozart, have mercy!
VENTICELLO 1   He speaks in Italian when excited!
VENTICELLO 2   German when not!
VENTICELLO 1   *Perdonami, Mozart!*
VENTICELLO 2   Pardon your assassin!

The Valet and the Cook walk to either side of the stage, and stand still. Pause. The Venticelli cross themselves, deeply shocked.

VENTICELLO 1   There was talk once before, you know.
VENTICELLO 2   Thirty-two years ago.
VENTICELLO 1   When Mozart was dying.
VENTICELLO 2   He claimed he'd been poisoned.
VENTICELLO 1   Some said he accused a man.
VENTICELLO 2   Some said that man was Salieri.
VENTICELLO 1   But no one believed it.
VENTICELLO 2   They *knew* what he died of!
VENTICELLO 1   Syphilis, surely.
VENTICELLO 2   Like everybody else.

Pause.

VENTICELLO 1   (*slyly*) But what if Mozart was right?
VENTICELLO 2   If he really *was* murdered?
VENTICELLO 1   And by him. Our First Kapellmeister!
VENTICELLO 2   Antonio Salieri!
VENTICELLO 1   It can't possibly be true.
VENTICELLO 2   It's not actually credible.
VENTICELLO 1   Because *why?*
VENTICELLO 2   Because why?
VENTICELLO 1 and VENTICELLO 2   *Why on earth would he do it?*
VENTICELLO 1   And why confess *now?*
VENTICELLO 2   After thirty-two years!
WHISPERERS   SALIERI!

SALIERI *Mozart! Mozart! Perdonami! ... Il tuo assassino ti chiede perdono!*

Pause. They look at him – then at each other.

VENTICELLO 1 What do you think?
VENTICELLO 2 What do you think?
VENTICELLO 1 I don't believe it!
VENTICELLO 2 *I* don't believe it!
VENTICELLO 1 All the same ...
VENTICELLO 2 Is it just possible?
VENTICELLO 1 and VENTICELLO 2 *(whispering) Did he do it after all?*
WHISPERERS SALIERI!

The Venticelli go off. The Valet and the Cook remain, on either side of the stage. Salieri swivels his wheelchair around and stares at us. We see a man of seventy in an old stained dressing-robe, shawled. He rises and squints at the Audience as if trying to see it.

*   *   *   *

Salieri's apartments

November 1823. The small hours.

SALIERI *(calling to Audience) Vi Saluto! Ombri del Futuro!* Antonio Salieri – *a vostro servizio!*

A clock outside in the street strikes three.

I can almost see you in your ranks – waiting for your turn to live. Ghosts of the Future! Be visible. I beg you. Be visible. Come to this dusty old room – this time, the smallest hours of dark November, 1823 – and be my Confessors! Will you not enter this place and stay with me till dawn? Just till dawn – till six o'clock!

WHISPERERS *Salieri! ... Salieri! ...*

The curtains slowly descend on the Citizens of Vienna. Faint images of long windows are projected on the silk.

5

SALIERI Can you hear them? Vienna is a City of Slander. Everyone tells tales here: even my servants. I keep only two now – (*He indicates them.*) – they've been with me ever since I came here, fifty years ago. The Keeper of the Razor: the Maker of the Cakes. One keeps me tidy, the other keeps me full. (*To them*) Leave me, both of you! Tonight I do not go to bed at all!

They react in surprise.

Return here tomorrow morning at six precisely – to shave, to feed your capricious master! (*He smiles at them both and claps his hands in gentle dismissal.*) *Via. Via, via, via! Grazie!*

They bow, bewildered, and leave the stage.

How surprised they are! . . . They'll be even more surprised tomorrow: indeed they will! (*He peers hard at the Audience, trying to see it.*) Oh, won't you appear? I need you – desperately! Those about to die implore you! What must I do to make you visible? Raise you up in the flesh to be my last, last Audience? . . . Does it take an Invocation? That's how it's always done in Opera! Ah yes, of course: that's it. An *Invocation*. The only way. (*He rises.*) Let me try to conjure you *now* – Ghosts of the distant Future – so I can see you.

He gets out of the wheelchair and huddles over to the fortepiano. He stands at the instrument and begins to sing in a high cracked voice, interrupting himself at the end of each sentence with figurations on the keyboard in the manner of a Recitativo Secco. During this the House Lights slowly come up to illuminate the Audience.

SALIERI (*singing*)
Ghosts of the Future!
Shades of Time to come!
So much more unavoidable than those of Time gone by!
Appear with what sympathy Incarnation may endow you!
Appear you –
The yet-to-be-born!

The yet-to-hate!
The yet-to-*kill*!
Appear – Posterity!

The light on the Audience reaches its maximum. It stays like this during all of the following.

(*Speaking again*) There. It worked. I can see you! That is the result of proper training. I was taught invocation by Chevalier Gluck, who was a true master at it. He had to be. In his day that is what people went to the opera for: the raising of Gods, and Ghosts . . . Nowadays, since Rossini became the rage, they prefer to watch the antics of hairdressers.

Pause.

Scusate. Invocation is an exhausting business. I need refreshment. (*He goes to the cake-stand.*) It's a little repellent, I admit – but actually the first sin I have to confess to you is Gluttony. Sticky gluttony at that. Infantine – Italian gluttony! The truth is that all my life I have never been able to conquer a lust for the sweetmeats of Northern Italy where I was born. From the ages of three to seventy-three my entire career has been conducted to the taste of almonds sprinkled with sifted sugar. (*Lustfully*) Milanese biscuits! Sienna macaroons! Snow dumplings with pistachio sauce! . . . Do not judge me too harshly for this. All men harbour patriotic feelings of some kind . . . My parents were Italian subjects of the Austrian Empire, a Lombardy merchant and his Lombardy wife. Their notion of Place was the tiny town of Legnago – which I could not wait to leave. Their notion of God was a superior Hapsburg Emperor inhabiting a Heaven only slightly further off than Vienna. All they asked of Him was to keep them forever unnoticed – preserved in mediocrity. My own requirements were very different.

Pause.

I wanted Fame. Not to deceive you. I wanted to *blaze*, like

7

a comet, across the firmament of Europe. Yet only in one especial way. Music. Absolute music! A note of music is either right or wrong – *absolutely*! Not even Time can alter that: music is God's art. (*Excited by the recollection*) Already when I was ten a spray of sounded notes would make me dizzy almost to falling! By twelve I was stumbling about the country-side, humming my arias and anthems to the Lord! My one desire was to join all the composers who had celebrated God's glory through the long Italian past! . . . Every Sunday I saw Him in Church, painted on the flaking wall. I don't mean Christ. The Christs of Lombardy are simpering sillies with lambkins on their sleeves. No: I mean an old candle-smoked God in a mulberry robe, staring at the world with dealer's eyes. Tradesmen had put him up there. Those eyes made bargains, real and irreversible. 'You give me so – I'll give you so! No more. No less!' (*He eats a sweet biscuit in his excitement.*) One night I went to see Him – and made a bargain with Him myself! I was a sober sixteen, filled with a desperate sense of right. I knelt before the God of Bargains, and I prayed with all my soul.

He kneels. The lights in the Audience go out slowly.

'Signore, let me be a Composer! Grant me sufficient Fame to enjoy it. In return I will live with virtue. I will be chaste. I will strive to better the lot of my fellows. And I will honour You with much music all the days of my life!' As I said Amen, I saw his eyes flare. (*As 'God'*) '*Bene.* Go forth Antonio. Serve Me and Mankind – and you will be blessed!' . . . '*Grazie!*' I called back. 'I am Your Servant for life!'

He gets to his feet again.

The very next day, a family friend suddenly appeared – out of the blue – took me off to Vienna and paid for me to study music!

Pause.

8

Shortly afterwards I met the Emperor of Austria, who favoured me. *Clearly my bargain had been accepted* !

Pause.

The same year I left Italy, a young prodigy was touring Europe. A miraculous virtuoso aged ten years. Wolfgang Amadeus Mozart.

Pause. He smiles at the Audience. Pause.

And now – Gracious Ladies! Obliging Gentlemen! I present to you – for one performance only – my last composition, entitled *The Death of Mozart*, or *Did I Do It?* . . . dedicated to Posterity on this – the last night of my life!

He bows deeply, undoing as he does so the buttons of his old dressing-robe. When he straightens himself – divesting himself of this drab outer garment and his cap – he is a young man in the prime of life, wearing a sky-blue coat and the elegant decent clothes of a successful composer of the seventeen-eighties.

* * * *

Transformation to the eighteenth century

Music sounds softly in the background: a serene piece for strings by Salieri. Servants enter. One takes away the dressing-robe and shawl; another places on the table a wig-stand bearing a powdered wig; a third brings on a chair and places it at the left, upstage.

At the back the blue curtains rise and part to show the Emperor Joseph II and his Court bathed in golden light, against a golden background of mirrors and an immense golden fireplace. His Majesty is seated, holding a rolled paper, listening to the music. Also listening are Count Von Strack; Count Orsini-Rosenberg; Baron Van Swieten; and an anonymous Priest dressed in a soutane. An old wigged Courtier enters and takes his place at the keyboard: Kapellmeister Bonno. Salieri takes his wig from the stand.

SALIERI   (*in a young man's voice, vigorous and confident*) The place

9

They approach him eagerly, from either side.

VENTICELLO 1   Mozart!

VENTICELLO 2   Mozart!

VENTICELLO 1 and VENTICELLO 2   *Mozart has come!*

SALIERI   These are my *Venticelli*. My 'Little Winds' as I call them. (*He gives each a coin from his pocket.*) The secret of successful living in a large city is always to know to the minute what is being done behind your back.

VENTICELLO 1   He's left Salzburg.

VENTICELLO 2   Means to give concerts.

VENTICELLO 1   Asking for subscribers.

SALIERI   I'd known of him for years, of course. Tales of his prowess were told all over Europe.

VENTICELLO 1   They say he wrote his first symphony at five.

VENTICELLO 2   I hear his first concerto at four.

VENTICELLO 1   A full opera at fourteen.

VENTICELLO 2   *Mitridate, King of Pontus.*

SALIERI   (*to them*) How old is he now?

VENTICELLO 2   Twenty-five.

SALIERI   (*carefully*) And how long is he remaining?

VENTICELLO 1   He's not departing.

VENTICELLO 2   He's here to stay.

The Venticelli glide off.

*   *   *   *

The Palace of Schönbrunn

Lights come up on the three stiff figures of Rosenberg, Strack and Van Swieten, standing upstage in the Light Box. The Chamberlain hands the paper he has received from the Emperor to the Director of the Opera. Salieri remains downstage.

STRACK   (*to Rosenberg*) You are required to commission a comic opera in German from Herr Mozart.

SALIERI   (*to Audience*) Johann Von Strack. Royal Chamberlain. A Court official to his collar bone.

ROSENBERG *(loftily)* Why in German? Italian is the only possible language for opera!

SALIERI Count Orsini-Rosenberg. Director of the Opera. Benevolent to all things Italian – especially myself.

STRACK *(stiffly)* The idea of a National Opera is dear to His Majesty's heart. He desires to hear pieces in good plain German.

VAN SWIETEN Yes, but why comic? It is not the function of music to be funny.

SALIERI Baron Van Swieten. Prefect of the Imperial Library. Ardent Freemason. Yet to find anything funny. Known for his enthusiasm for old-fashioned music as 'Lord Fugue'.

VAN SWIETEN I heard last week a remarkable *serious* opera from Mozart: *Idomeneo, King of Crete.*

ROSENBERG I heard that too. A young fellow trying to impress beyond his abilities. Too much spice. Too many notes.

STRACK *(firmly, to Rosenberg)* Nevertheless, kindly convey the commission to him today.

ROSENBERG *(taking the paper reluctantly)* I believe we are going to have trouble with this young man.

Rosenberg leaves the Light Box and strolls down the stage to Salieri.

He was a child prodigy. That always spells trouble. His father is Leopold Mozart, a pedantic Salzburg musician in the service of the Archbishop. He dragged the boy endlessly round Europe making him play the keyboard blindfold, with one finger, and that sort of thing. *(To Salieri)* All prodigies are hateful – *non è vero, Compositore?*

SALIERI *Divengono sempre sterili con gli anni.*

ROSENBERG *Precisamente. Precisamente.*

STRACK *(calling suspiciously)* What are you saying?

ROSENBERG *(airily)* Nothing, Herr Chamberlain! . . . *Niente,* Signor Pomposo! . . .

He strolls on out. Strack strides off irritated. Van Swieten now comes downstage.

13

VAN SWIETEN   We meet tomorrow, I believe, on your committee to devise pensions for old musicians.

SALIERI   (*deferentially*) It's most gracious of you to attend, Baron.

VAN SWIETEN   You're a worthy man, Salieri. You should join our Brotherhood of Masons. We would welcome you warmly.

SALIERI   I would be honoured, Baron!

VAN SWIETEN   If you wished I could arrange initiation into my Lodge.

SALIERI   That would be more than my due.

VAN SWIETEN   Nonsense. We embrace men of talent of all conditions. I may invite young Mozart also: dependent on the impression he makes.

SALIERI   (*bowing*) Of course, Baron.

Van Swieten goes out.

(*to Audience*) Honour indeed. In those days almost every man of influence in Vienna was a Mason – and the Baron's Lodge by far the most fashionable. As for young Mozart, I confess I was alarmed by his coming. He was praised altogether too much.

The Venticelli hurry in from either side.

VENTICELLO 1   Such gaiety of spirit!

VENTICELLO 2   Such ease of manner!

VENTICELLO 1   Such natural charm!

SALIERI   (*to the Venticelli*) Really? Where does he live?

VENTICELLO 1   Peter Platz.

VENTICELLO 2   Number eleven.

VENTICELLO 1   The landlady is Madame Weber.

VENTICELLO 2   A real bitch.

VENTICELLO 1   Takes in male lodgers, and has a tribe of daughters.

VENTICELLO 2   Mozart was engaged to one of them before.

VENTICELLO 1   A soprano called Aloysia.

VENTICELLO 2   She jilted him.

VENTICELLO 1   Now he's after another sister.

VENTICELLO 2   Constanze!

SALIERI   You mean he was actually engaged to one sister and now wants to marry another?

VENTICELLO 1 and VENTICELLO 2   (*together*) Exactly!

VENTICELLO 1   Her mother's pushing marriage.

VENTICELLO 2   His *father* isn't!

VENTICELLO 1   Daddy is worried sick!

VENTICELLO 2   Writes him every day from Salzburg!

SALIERI   (*to them*) I want to meet him.

VENTICELLO 1   He'll be at the Baroness Waldstädten's tomorrow night.

SALIERI   *Grazie.*

VENTICELLO 2   Some of his music is to be played.

SALIERI   (*to both*) *Restiamo in contatto.*

VENTICELLO 1 and VENTICELLO 2   *Certamente, Signore!*

They go off.

SALIERI   (*to Audience*) So to the Baroness Waldstädten's I went. That night changed my life.

*   *   *   *

The Library of the Baroness Waldstädten

In the Light Box, two elegantly curtained windows surrounded by handsome subdued wallpaper.

Two Servants bring on a large table loaded with cakes and desserts. Two more carry on a grand high-backed wing-chair, which they place ceremoniously downstage at the left.

SALIERI   (*to Audience*) I entered the library to take first a little refreshment. My generous hostess always put out the most delicious confections in that room whenever she knew I was coming. *Sorbetti – caramelli –* and most especially a miraculous *crema al mascarpone* – which is simply cream cheese mixed with granulated sugar and suffused with rum – that was totally irresistible!

15

He takes a little bowl of it from the cake-stand and sits in the wing-chair, facing out front. Thus seated, he is invisible to anyone entering from upstage.

I had just sat down in a high-backed chair to consume this paradisal dish – unobservable as it happened to anyone who might come in.

Offstage, noises are heard.

CONSTANZE (*off*) Squeak! Squeak! Squeak!

Constanze runs on from upstage : a pretty girl in her early twenties, full of high spirits. At this second she is pretending to be a mouse. She runs across the stage in her gay party dress, and hides under the fortepiano.
  Suddenly a small, pallid, large-eyed man in a showy wig and a showy set of clothes runs in after her and freezes – centre – as a cat would freeze, hunting a mouse. This is Wolfgang Amadeus Mozart.
  As we get to know him through his next scenes, we discover several things about him : he is an extremely restless man, his hands and feet in almost continuous motion; his voice is light and high; and he is possessed of an unforgettable giggle – piercing and infantile.

MOZART Miaouw!
CONSTANZE (*betraying where she is*) Squeak!
MOZART Miaouw! Miaouw! Miaouw!

The composer drops on all fours and, wrinkling his face, begins spitting and stalking his prey. The mouse – giggling with excitement – breaks her cover and dashes across the floor. The cat pursues. Almost at the chair where Salieri sits concealed, the mouse turns at bay. The cat stalks her – nearer and nearer – in its knee-breeches and elaborate coat.

MOZART I'm going to pounce-bounce! I'm going to scrunch-munch! I'm going to chewpoo my little mouse-wouse! I'm going to tear her to bits with my paws-claws!
CONSTANZE No!
MOZART Paws-claws,
      paws-claws,

16

paws-claws! OHH!...

He falls on her. She screams.

SALIERI   (*to Audience*) Before I could rise, it had become difficult
to do so.

MOZART   I'm going to bite you in half with my fangs-wangs!
My little Stanzerl-wanzerl-banzerl!

She giggles delightedly, lying prone beneath him.

You're trembling!... I think you're frightened of puss-wuss!
... I think you're scared to death! (*Intimately*) I think you're
going to shit yourself.

She squeals, but is not really shocked.

In a moment it's going to be on the floor!

CONSTANZE   Ssh! Someone'll hear you!

He imitates the noise of a fart.

Stop it, Wolferl! Ssh!

MOZART   All nasty and smelly on the floor.

CONSTANZE   No!

MOZART   Here it comes now! I can hear it *coming*!... Oh what
a melancholy note! Something's dropping from your boat!

Another fart noise, slower. Constanze shrieks with amusement.

CONSTANZE   Stop it now! It's stupid! Really *stupid!*

Salieri sits appalled.

MOZART   Hey – Hey – what's Trazom!

CONSTANZE   What?

MOZART   T R A Z O M. What's that mean?

CONSTANZE   How should *I* know?

MOZART   It's Mozart spelt backwards – shit-wit! If you ever
married me, you'd be Constanze Trazom.

CONSTANZE   No, I wouldn't.

MOZART   Yes, you would. Because I'd want everything back-

17

wards once I was married. I'd want to lick my wife's arse instead of her face.

CONSTANZE   You're not going to lick anything at this rate. Your father's never going to give his consent to us.

The sense of fun deserts him instantly.

MOZART   And who cares about his consent?

CONSTANZE   *You* do. You care very much. You wouldn't do it without it.

MOZART   Wouldn't I?

CONSTANZE   No, you wouldn't. Because you're too scared of him. I know what he says about me. (*Solemn voice*) 'If you marry that dreadful girl, you'll end up lying on straw with beggars for children.'

MOZART   (*impulsively*) Marry me!

CONSTANZE   Don't be silly.

MOZART   Marry me!

CONSTANZE   Are you serious?

MOZART   (*defiantly*) Yes! . . . Answer me this minute: yes or no! Say yes, then I can go home, climb into bed – shit over the mattress and shout 'I *did* it!'

He rolls on top of her delightedly, uttering his high whinnying giggle. The Major-Domo of the house stalks in, upstage.

MAJOR-DOMO   (*imperviously*) Her Ladyship is ready to commence.

MOZART   Ah! . . . Yes! . . . Good! (*He picks himself up, embarrassed, and helps Constanze to rise. With an attempt at dignity*) Come, my dear. The music waits!

CONSTANZE   (*suppressing giggles*) Oh, by all means – Herr Trazom!

He takes her arm. They prance off together, followed by the disapproving Major-Domo.

SALIERI   (*shaken: to Audience*) And then, right away, the concert began. I heard it through the door – some Serenade: at first only vaguely – too horrified to attend. But presently the sound insisted – a solemn Adagio in E flat.

The Adagio from the Serenade for Thirteen Wind Instruments (K.361) begins to sound. Quietly and quite slowly, seated in the wing-chair, Salieri speaks over the music.

It started simply enough: just a pulse in the lowest registers – bassoons and basset horns – like a rusty squeezebox. It would have been comic except for the slowness, which gave it instead a sort of serenity. And then suddenly, high above it, sounded a single note on the oboe.

We hear it.

It hung there unwavering – piercing me through – till breath could hold it no longer, and a clarinet withdrew it out of me, and sweetened it into a phrase of such delight it had me trembling. The light flickered in the room. My eyes clouded! (*With ever-increasing emotion and vigour*) The squeezebox groaned louder, and over it the higher instruments wailed and warbled, throwing lines of sound around me – long lines of pain around and through me – Ah, the pain! Pain as I had never known it. I called up to my sharp old God '*What is this? . . . What?!*' But the squeezebox went on and on, and the pain cut deeper into my shaking head until suddenly I was running –

He bolts out of the chair and runs across the stage in a fever, to centre. Behind him in the Light Box the Library fades into a street scene at night: small houses under a rent sky. The music continues, fainter, underneath.

– dashing through the side-door, stumbling downstairs into the street, into the cold night, gasping for life. (*Calling up in agony*) '*What? What is this? Tell me, Signore!* What is this *pain*? What is this *need* in the sound? Forever unfulfillable yet fulfilling him who hears it, utterly. Is it *Your* need? *Can it be Yours? . . .*'

19

Pause.

Dimly the music sounded from the salon above. Dimly the stars shone on the empty street. I was suddenly frightened. It seemed to me I had heard a voice of God – and that it issued from a creature whose own voice I had also heard – and it was the voice of an obscene child!

Light change. The street scene fades.

*　　*　　*　　*

Salieri's apartments

It remains dark.

SALIERI　I ran home and buried my fear in work. More pupils – till there were thirty and forty. More committees toiling long hours to help musicians! More motets and anthems to God's glory. And at night I prayed for just one thing. (*He kneels desperately.*) 'Let your voice enter *me*! Let *me* be your conduct! . . . *Let* me!' (*Pause. He rises.*) As for Mozart, I avoided meeting him – and sent out my Little Winds for whatever scores of his could be found.

The Venticelli come in with manuscripts. Salieri sits at the fortepiano, and they show him the music alternately, as Servants unobtrusively remove the Waldstädten table and wing-chair.

VENTICELLO 1　Six fortepiano sonatas composed in Munich.
SALIERI　Clever.
VENTICELLO 2　Two in Mannheim.
SALIERI　They were all clever.
VENTICELLO 1　A Parisian Symphony.
SALIERI　(*to Audience*) And yet they seemed to me completely empty!
VENTICELLO 1　A Divertimento in D.
SALIERI　Same.
VENTICELLO 2　A Cassazione in G.

SALIERI Conventional.

VENTICELLO 1 A Grand Litany in E Flat.

SALIERI Even boring. (*To Audience*) The productions of a precocious youngster – Leopold Mozart's swanky son – nothing more. That Serenade was obviously an exception in his work: the sort of accident which might visit any composer on a lucky day!

The Venticelli go off with the music.

Had I in fact been simply taken by surprise that the filthy creature could write music at all?... Suddenly I felt immensely cheered! I would seek him out and welcome him myself to Vienna!

*   *   *   *

The Palace of Schönbrunn

Quick light change. The Emperor is revealed standing in bright light before the gilded mirrors and the fireplace, attended by Chamberlain Strack. His Majesty is a dapper, cheerful figure, aged forty, largely pleased with himself and the world. Downstage, from opposite sides, Van Swieten and Rosenberg hurry on.

JOSEPH Fêtes and fireworks, gentlemen! Mozart is here! He's waiting below!

All bow.

ALL Majesty!

JOSEPH *Je suis follement impatient!*

SALIERI (*to Audience*) The Emperor Joseph the Second of Austria. Son of Maria Theresa. Brother of Marie Antoinette. Adorer of music – provided that it made no demands upon the royal brain. (*To the Emperor, deferentially*) Majesty, I have written a little march in Mozart's honour. May I play it as he comes in?

JOSEPH By all means, Court Composer. What a delightful idea!

21

Have you met him yet?

SALIERI   Not yet, Majesty.

JOSEPH   Fêtes and fireworks, what fun! Strack, bring him up at once.

Strack goes off. The Emperor comes on to the stage proper.

Mon Dieu, I wish we could have a competition! Mozart against some other virtuoso. Two keyboards in contest. Wouldn't that be fun, Baron?

VAN SWIETEN   *(stiffly)* Not to me, Majesty. In my view, musicians are not horses to be run against one another.

Slight pause.

JOSEPH   Ah. Well – there it is.

Strack returns.

STRACK   Herr Mozart, Majesty.

JOSEPH   Ah! Splendid! . . . *(Conspiratorially he signs to Salieri, who moves quickly to the fortepiano.)* Court Composer – allons! *(To Strack)* Admit him, please.

Instantly Salieri sits at the instrument and strikes up his March on the keyboard. At the same moment Mozart struts in, wearing an extremely ornate surcoat, with dress-sword.

The Emperor stands downstage, centre, his back to the Audience, and as Mozart approaches he signs to him to halt and listen. Bewildered, Mozart does so – becoming aware of Salieri playing his March of Welcome. It is an extremely banal piece, vaguely – but only vaguely – reminiscent of another march to become very famous later on. All stand frozen in attitudes of listening, until Salieri comes to a finish. Applause.

JOSEPH   *(to Salieri)* Charming . . . Comme d'habitude! *(He turns and extends his hand to be kissed.)* Mozart.

Mozart approaches and kneels extravagantly.

MOZART   Majesty! Your Majesty's humble slave! Let me kiss your royal hand a hundred thousand times!

He kisses it greedily, over and over, until its owner withdraws it in embarrassment.

JOSEPH   *Non, non, s'il vous plaît!* A little less enthusiasm, I beg you. Come sir, *levez-vous!* (*He assists Mozart to rise.*) You will not recall it, but the last time we met you were also on the floor! My sister remembers it to this day. This young man – all of six years old, mind you – slipped on the floor at Schönbrunn – came a nasty purler on his little head . . . Have I told you this before?

ROSENBERG   (*hastily*) No, Majesty!

STRACK   (*hastily*) No, Majesty!

SALIERI   (*hastily*) No, Majesty!

JOSEPH   Well, my sister Antoinette runs forward and picks him up herself. And do you know what he does? Jumps right into her arms – hoopla, just like that! – kisses her on both cheeks and says 'Will you marry me: yes or no?'

The Courtiers laugh politely. Mozart emits his high-pitched giggle. The Emperor is clearly startled by it.

I do not mean to embarrass you, Herr Mozart. You know everyone here, surely?

MOZART   Yes, Sire. (*Bowing elaborately to Rosenberg*) Herr Director! (*To Van Swieten*) Herr Prefect.

JOSEPH   But not, I think, our esteemed Court Composer! . . . A most serious omission! No one who cares for art can afford not to know Herr Salieri. He wrote that exquisite little March of Welcome for you.

SALIERI   It was a trifle, Majesty.

JOSEPH   Nevertheless . . .

MOZART   (*to Salieri*) I'm overwhelmed, Signore!

JOSEPH   Ideas simply pour out of him – don't they, Strack?

STRACK   Endlessly, sire. (*As if tipping him*) Well done, Salieri.

JOSEPH   Let it be my pleasure then to introduce you! Court Composer Salieri – Herr Mozart of Salzburg!

SALIERI   (*sleekly, to Mozart*) *Finalmente. Che gioia. Che diletto straordinario.*

He gives him a prim bow and presents the copy of his music to the other composer, who accepts it with a flood of Italian.

MOZART   *Grazie Signore! Mille milione di benvenuti! Sono commosso! E` un onore eccezionale incontrarla! Compositore brillante e famosissimo!*

He makes an elaborate and showy bow in return.

SALIERI   (*dryly*) *Grazie.*

JOSEPH   Tell me, Mozart, have you received our commission for the opera?

MOZART   Indeed I have, Majesty! I am so grateful I can hardly speak! . . . I swear to you that you will have the best – the most perfect entertainment ever offered a monarch. I've already found a libretto.

ROSENBERG   (*startled*) Have you? I didn't hear of this!

MOZART   Forgive me, Herr Director, I entirely omitted to tell you.

ROSENBERG   May I ask why?

MOZART   It didn't seem very important.

ROSENBERG   Not important?

MOZART   Not really, no.

ROSENBERG   (*irritated*) It is important to *me*, Herr Mozart.

MOZART   (*embarrassed*) Yes, I see that. Of course.

ROSENBERG   And who, pray, is it by?

MOZART   Stephanie.

ROSENBERG   A most unpleasant man.

MOZART   But a brilliant writer.

ROSENBERG   Do you think?

MOZART   The story is really amusing, Majesty. The whole plot is set in a – (*He giggles*) – in a . . . It's set in a . . .

JOSEPH   (*eagerly*) Where? Where is it set?

MOZART   It's – it's – rather saucy, Majesty!

JOSEPH   Yes, yes! Where?

MOZART   Well it's actually set in a *seraglio*.

JOSEPH   A what?

MOZART   A pasha's harem. (*He giggles wildly.*)

ROSENBERG   And you imagine that is a suitable subject for performance at a National Theatre?

MOZART   (*in a panic*) Yes! No! Yes, I mean yes, yes I do. Why not? It's very funny, it's amusing . . . on my honour – Majesty – there's nothing offensive in it. Nothing offensive in the world. It's full of proper German virtues, I swear it! . . .

SALIERI   (*blandly*) *Scusate, Signore*, but what are those? Being a foreigner I'm not sure.

JOSEPH   You are being *cattivo*, Court Composer.

SALIERI   Not at all, Majesty.

JOSEPH   Come then, Mozart. Name us a proper German virtue!

MOZART   Love, Sire. I have yet to see that expressed in any opera.

VAN SWIETEN   Well answered, Mozart.

SALIERI   (*smiling*) *Scusate*. I was under the impression one rarely saw anything *else* expressed in opera.

MOZART   I mean manly love, Signore. Not male sopranos screeching. Or stupid couples rolling their eyes. All that absurd Italian rubbish.

Pause. Tension.

I mean the real thing.

JOSEPH   And do you know the real thing yourself, Herr Mozart?

MOZART   Under your pardon, I think I do, Majesty. (*He gives a short giggle.*)

JOSEPH   Bravo. When do you think it will be done?

MOZART   The first act is already finished.

JOSEPH   But it can't be more than two weeks since you started!

MOZART   Composing is not hard when you have the right audience to please, Sire.

VAN SWIETEN   A charming reply, Majesty.

JOSEPH   Indeed, Baron. Fêtes and fireworks! I see we are going to have fêtes and fireworks! *Au revoir, Monsieur Mozart. Soyez bienvenu à la court.*

MOZART   (*with expert rapidity*) *Majesté! – je suis comblé d'honneur*

25

d'être accepté dans la maison du Père de tous les musiciens! Servir un monarque aussi plein de discernement que votre Majesté, c'est un honneur qui dépasse le sommet de mes dûs!

A pause. The Emperor is taken aback by this flood of French.

JOSEPH Ah. Well – there it is. I'll leave you gentlemen to get better acquainted.

SALIERI Good day, Majesty.

MOZART *Votre Majesté.*

They both bow. Joseph goes out.

ROSENBERG Good day to you.

STRACK Good day.

They follow the King.

VAN SWIETEN (*warmly shaking his hand*) Welcome, Mozart. I shall see much more of you. Depend on it!

MOZART Thank you.

He bows. The Baron goes. Mozart and Salieri are left alone.

SALIERI *Bene.*

MOZART *Bene.*

SALIERI I too wish you success with your opera.

MOZART I'll have it. It's going to be superb. I must tell you I have already found the most excellent singer for the leading part.

SALIERI Oh: who is that?

MOZART Her name is Cavalieri. Katherina Cavalieri. She's really German, but she thinks it will advance her career if she sports an Italian name.

SALIERI She's quite right. It was my idea. She is in fact my prize pupil. Actually she's a very innocent child. Silly in the way of young singers – but, you know, she's only twenty.

Without emphasis Mozart freezes his movements and Salieri takes one easy step forward to make a fluent aside.

(*to Audience*) I had kept my hands off Katherina. Yes! But, I could not bear to think of anyone else's upon her – least of all his!

MOZART (*unfreezing*) You're a good fellow, Salieri! And that's a jolly little thing you wrote for me.

SALIERI It was my pleasure.

MOZART Let's see if I can remember it. May I?

SALIERI By all means. It's yours.

MOZART *Grazie*, Signore.

Mozart tosses the manuscript on to the lid of the fortepiano where he cannot see it, sits at the instrument, and plays Salieri's March of Welcome perfectly from memory – at first slowly, recalling it – but on the reprise of the tune, very much faster.

The rest is just the same, isn't it? (*He finishes it with insolent speed.*)

SALIERI You have a remarkable memory.

MOZART (*delighted with himself*) *Grazie ancora*, Signore! (*He plays the opening seven bars again, but this time stops on the interval of the Fourth, and sounds it again with displeasure.*) It doesn't really work, that Fourth – does it? . . . Let's try the Third above . . . (*He does so – and smiles happily.*) Ah yes! . . . Good! . . .

He repeats the new interval, leading up to it smartly with the well-known military-trumpet arpeggio which characterizes the celebrated March from The Marriage of Figaro, '*Non più andrai*'. *Then, using the interval – tentatively – delicately – one note at a time, in the treble – he steals into the famous tune itself.*

On and on he plays, improvizing happily what is virtually the march we know now, laughing gleefully each time he comes to the amended interval of a Third. Salieri watches him with an answering smile painted on his face.

Mozart's playing grows more and more exhibitionistic – revealing to the Audience the formidable virtuoso he is. The whole time he himself remains totally oblivious to the offence he is giving. Finally he finishes the March with a series of triumphant flourishes and chords!

An ominous pause.

SALIERI *Scusate.* I must go.

MOZART Really? (*Springing up and indicating the keyboard*) Why don't *you* try a Variation?

SALIERI Thank you, but I must attend on the Emperor.

MOZART Ah.

SALIERI It has been delightful to meet you.

MOZART For me too! . . . And thanks for the March!

Mozart picks up the manuscript from the top of the fortepiano and marches happily offstage.
    A slight pause.
    Salieri moves towards the Audience. The lights go down around him.

SALIERI (*to Audience*) Was it then – so early – that I began to have thoughts of murder? . . . Of course not: at least not in Life. In Art it was a different matter. I decided I would compose a huge tragic opera: something to astonish the world! – and I knew my theme. I would set the Legend of Danaius, who, for a monstrous crime was chained to a rock for eternity – his head repeatedly struck by lightning! Wickedly I saw Mozart in that position. In reality the man was in no danger at all . . . Not yet.

*   *   *   *

The first performance of **The Abduction from the Seraglio**

The light changes, and the stage instantly turns into an eighteenth-century theatre. The backdrop projection shows a line of softly gleaming chandeliers.

The Servants bring in chairs and benches. Upon them, facing the Audience and regarding it as if watching an opera, sit the Emperor Joseph, Strack, Rosenberg and Van Swieten.

Next to them: Kapellmeister Bonno and Teresa Salieri. A little behind them: Constanze. Behind her: Citizens of Vienna.

SALIERI The first performance of *The Abduction from the Seraglio*. The German expression of manly love.

Mozart comes on briskly, wearing a gaudy new coat and a new powdered wig. He struts quickly to the fortepiano, sits at it and mimes conducting. Salieri sits nearby, next to his wife, and watches Mozart intently.

He himself contrived to wear for the occasion an even more vulgar coat than usual. As for the music, it matched the coat completely. For my dear pupil Katherina Cavalieri he had written quite simply the showiest aria I'd ever heard.

Faintly we hear the whizzing scale passages for soprano which end the aria 'Marten Aller Arten'.

Ten minutes of scales and ornaments, amounting in sum to a vast emptiness. So ridiculous was the piece in fact – so much what might be demanded by a foolish young soprano – that I knew precisely what Mozart must have demanded in return for it.

The final orchestral chords of the aria. Silence. No one moves.

Although engaged to be married, *he'd had her!* I knew that beyond any doubt. (*Bluntly*) The creature had had my darling girl.

Loudly we hear the brilliant Turkish Finale of 'Seraglio'. Great applause from those watching. Mozart jumps to his feet and acknowledges it. The Emperor rises – as do all – and gestures graciously to the 'stage' in invitation. Katherina Cavalieri runs on in her costume, all plumes and flounces, to renewed cheering and clapping. She curtseys to the Emperor – is kissed by Salieri – presented to his wife – curtseys again to Mozart and, flushed with triumph, moves to one side.

In the ensuing brief silence Constanze rushes down from the back, wildly excited. She flings herself on Mozart, not even noticing the Emperor.

29

CONSTANZE   Oh, well done, lovey! ... Well done, pussy-wussy! ...

Mozart indicates the proximity of His Majesty.

Oh! ... 'Scuse *me!* (*She curtseys in embarrassment.*)

MOZART   Majesty, may I present my fiancée, Fraulein Weber.

JOSEPH   *Enchanté, Fraulein.*

CONSTANZE   Your Majesty!

MOZART   Constanze is a singer herself.

JOSEPH   Indeed?

CONSTANZE   (*embarrassed*) I'm not at all, Majesty. Don't be silly, Wolfgang!

JOSEPH   So, Mozart – a good effort. Decidedly that. A good effort.

MOZART   Did you really like it, Sire?

JOSEPH   I thought it was most interesting. Yes, indeed. A trifle – how shall one say? (*To Rosenberg*) How shall one say, Director?

ROSENBERG   (*subserviently*) Too many notes, Your Majesty?

JOSEPH   Very well put. Too many notes.

MOZART   I don't understand.

JOSEPH   My dear fellow, don't take it too hard. There are in fact only so many notes the ear can hear in the course of an evening. I think I'm right in saying that, aren't I, Court Composer.

SALIERI   (*uncomfortably*) Well yes, I would say yes, on the whole, yes, Majesty.

JOSEPH   There you are. It's clever. It's German. It's quality work. And there are simply too many notes. Do you see?

MOZART   There are just as many notes, Majesty, neither more nor less, as are required.

Pause.

JOSEPH   Ah ... Well, there it is. (*He goes off abruptly, followed by Rosenberg and Strack.*)

MOZART   (*nervous*) Is he angry?

SALIERI   Not at all. He respects you for your views.

MOZART   (*nervously*) I hope so . . . What did you think yourself, sir? Did you care for the piece at all?

SALIERI   Yes, of course, Mozart – at its best it is truly charming.

MOZART   And at other times?

SALIERI   (*smoothly*) Well, just occasionally at other times – in Katherina's aria, for example – it was a little excessive.

MOZART   Katherina is an excessive girl. In fact she's insatiable.

SALIERI   All the same, as my revered teacher the Chevalier Gluck used to say to me – one must avoid music that smells of music.

MOZART   What does that mean?

SALIERI   Music which makes one aware too much of the virtuosity of the composer.

MOZART   Gluck is absurd.

SALIERI   What do you say?

MOZART   He's talked all his life about modernizing opera, but creates people so lofty they sound as though they shit marble.

Constanze gives a little scream of shock.

CONSTANZE   Oh, 'scuse me! . . .

MOZART   (*breaking out*) No, but it's too much! Gluck says! Gluck says! Chevalier Gluck! . . . What's Chevalier? I'm a Chevalier. The Pope made me a Chevalier when I was still wetting my bed.

CONSTANZE   Wolferl!

MOZART   Anyway it's ridiculous. Only stupid farts use titles.

SALIERI   (*blandly*) Such as Court Composer?

MOZART   What? . . . (*Realizing*) Ah. Oh. Ha. Ha. Well! . . . My father's right again. He always tells me I should padlock my mouth . . . Actually, I shouldn't speak at all!

SALIERI   (*soothingly*) Nonsense. I'm just being what the Emperor would call *cattivo*. Won't you introduce me to your charming fiancée?

MOZART   Oh, of course! Constanze, this is Herr Court Composer Salieri, Fraulein Weber.

SALIERI   (*bowing*) Delighted, *cara Fraulein*.

CONSTANZE   (*bobbing*) How do you do, Excellency?

SALIERI   You are the sister of Aloysia Weber, the soprano, are you not?

CONSTANZE   I am, Excellency.

SALIERI   A beauty herself, but you exceed her by far, if I may observe.

CONSTANZE   Oh, thank you!

SALIERI   May I ask when you marry?

MOZART   (*nervously*) We have to secure my father's consent. He's an excellent man – a wonderful man – but in some ways a little stubborn.

SALIERI   Excuse me, but how old are you?

MOZART   Twenty-six.

SALIERI   Then your father's consent is scarcely indispensable.

CONSTANZE   (*to Mozart*) You see?

MOZART   (*uncomfortably*) Well no, it's not *indispensable* – of course not! . . .

SALIERI   My advice to you is to marry and be happy. You have found – it's quite obvious – *un tesoro raro*!

CONSTANZE   Ta very much.

SALIERI   (*he kisses Constanze's hand. She is delighted.*) Goodnight to you both.

CONSTANZE   Goodnight, Excellency!

MOZART   Goodnight, sir. And thank you . . . Come, Stanzerl.

They depart delightedly. He watches them go.

SALIERI   (*to Audience*) As I watched her walk away on the arm of the Creature, I felt the lightning thought strike – 'Have her! Her for Katherina!' . . . Abomination! . . . Never in my life had I entertained a notion so sinful!

Light change: the eighteenth century fades.

The Venticelli come on merrily, as if from some celebration. One holds a bottle; the other a glass.

VENTICELLO 1   They're married.

SALIERI   (*to them*) What?

VENTICELLO 2   Mozart and Weber – married!

SALIERI   Really?

VENTICELLO 1   His father will be furious!

VENTICELLO 2   They didn't even wait for his consent!

SALIERI   Have they set up house?

VENTICELLO 1   Wipplingerstrasse.

VENTICELLO 2   Number twelve.

VENTICELLO 1   Not bad.

VENTICELLO 2   Considering they've no money.

SALIERI   Is that really true?

VENTICELLO 1   He's wildly extravagant.

VENTICELLO 2   Lives way beyond his means.

SALIERI   But he has pupils.

VENTICELLO 1   Only three.

SALIERI   (*to them*) Why so few?

VENTICELLO 1   He's embarrassing.

VENTICELLO 2   Makes scenes.

VENTICELLO 1   Makes enemies.

VENTICELLO 2   Even Strack, whom he cultivates.

SALIERI   Chamberlain Strack?

VENTICELLO 1   Only last night.

VENTICELLO 2   At Kapellmeister Bonno's.

*   *   *   *

Bonno's house

Instant light change. Mozart comes in with Strack. He is high on wine, and holding a glass. The Venticelli join the scene, but still talk out of it to Salieri. One of them fills Mozart's glass.

MOZART   Seven months in this city and not one job! I'm not to be tried again, is that it?

STRACK   Of course not.

MOZART   I know what goes on – and so do you. Vienna is completely in the hands of foreigners. Worthless wops like *Kapellmeister Bonno!*

STRACK   Please! You're in the man's house!

33

MOZART   Court Composer *Salieri*!

STRACK   Hush!

MOZART   Did you see his last opera? – *The Chimney Sweep*? . . . Did you?

STRACK   Of course I did.

MOZART   Dogshit. Dried dogshit.

STRACK   (*outraged*) I beg your pardon!

Mozart goes to the fortepiano and thumps on it monotonously.

MOZART   (*singing*) Pom-pom, pom-pom, pom-pom, pom-pom! Tonic and dominant, tonic and dominant from here to resurrection! Not one interesting modulation all night. Salieri is a musical idiot!

STRACK   Please!

VENTICELLO 1   (*to Salieri*) He'd had too much to drink.

VENTICELLO 2   He often has.

MOZART   Why are Italians so terrified by the slightest complexity in music? Show them one chromatic passage and they *faint*! . . . 'Oh how sick!' 'How morbid!' (*Falsetto*) *Morboso*! . . . *Nervoso*! . . . *Ohimè*! . . . *No wonder the music at this court is so dreary.*

STRACK   Lower your voice.

MOZART   Lower your breeches! . . . That's just a joke – just a joke!

Unobserved by him Count Rosenberg has entered upstage and is suddenly standing between the Venticelli, listening. He wears a waistcoat of bright green silk, and an expression of supercilious interest. Mozart sees him. A pause.

(*pleasantly, to Rosenberg*) You look like a toad . . . I mean you're goggling like a toad. (*He giggles.*)

ROSENBERG   (*blandly*) You would do best to retire tonight, for your own sake.

MOZART   Salieri has fifty pupils. I have three. How am I to live? I'm a married man now! . . . Of course I realize you don't concern yourselves with *money* in these exalted circles. All the same, did you know behind his back His Majesty is known as

Kaiser Keep it? (*He giggles wildly.*)

STRACK   *Mozart!*

He stops.

MOZART   I shouldn't have said that, should I? Forgive me. It was just a joke. Another joke!... I can't help myself!... We're all friends here, aren't we?

Strack and Rosenberg glare at him. Then Strack leaves abruptly, much offended.

MOZART   What's wrong with him?

ROSENBERG   Goodnight.

He turns to go.

MOZART   No, no, no – please! (*He grabs the Director's arm.*) Your hand please, first!

Unwillingly Rosenberg gives him his hand. Mozart kisses it.

(*humbly*) Give me a Post, sir.

ROSENBERG   That is not in my power, Mozart.

MOZART   The Princess Elizabeth is looking for an Instructor. One word from you could secure it for me.

ROSENBERG   I regret that is solely in the recommendation of Court Composer Salieri. (*He disengages himself.*)

MOZART   Do you know I am better than any musician in Vienna?... Do you?

Rosenberg leaves. Mozart calls after him.

Foppy-wops – I'm *sick* of them! Foppy-wops... (*Suddenly he giggles to himself, like a child.*) Foppy – poppy – snoppy – toppy – hoppy ... wops!

And hops offstage.

SALIERI   (*watching him go*) Barely one month later, that thought of revenge became more than thought.

*   *   *   *

35

The Waldstädten Library

Two simultaneous shouts bring up the lights. Against the handsome wallpaper stand three masked figures: Constanze, flanked on either side by the Venticelli. All three are guests at a party, and are playing a game of forfeits.

Two servants stand frozen, holding the large wing-chair between them. Two more hold the big table of sweetmeats.

VENTICELLO 1   Forfeit! . . . Forfeit! . . .

VENTICELLO 2   Forfeit, Stanzerl! You've got to forfeit!

CONSTANZE   I won't.

VENTICELLO 1   You have to.

VENTICELLO 2   It's the game.

The servants unfreeze and set down the furniture. Salieri moves to the wing-chair and sits.

SALIERI   (*to Audience*) Once again – believe it or not – I was in the same concealing chair in the Baroness's Library – (*taking a cup from the little table*) – and consuming the same delicious dessert.

VENTICELLO 1   You lost – now there's the penalty!

SALIERI   (*to Audience*) A party celebrating the New Year's Eve. I was on my own – my dear spouse Teresa visiting her parents in Italy.

CONSTANZE   Well, *what*? . . . What is it?

Venticello 1 snatches up an old-fashioned round ruler from off the fortepiano.

VENTICELLO 1   I want to measure your calves.

CONSTANZE   Oooo!

VENTICELLO 1   Well?

CONSTANZE   Definitely not! You cheeky bugger!

VENTICELLO 1   Now come on!

VENTICELLO 2   You've got to let him, Stanzerl. All's fair in love and forfeits.

CONSTANZE   No it isn't – so you can both buzz off!

VENTICELLO 1   If you don't let me, you won't be allowed to play again.

CONSTANZE   Well choose something else.

VENTICELLO 1   I've chosen that. Now get up on the table. Quick, quick! *Allez-oop!* (*Gleefully he shifts the plates of sweetmeats from the table.*)

CONSTANZE   Quick, then! . . . Before anyone sees!

The two masked men lift the shrieking masked girl up on to the table.

VENTICELLO 1   Hold her, Friedrich.

CONSTANZE   I don't have to be held, thank you!

VENTICELLO 2   Yes, you do: that's part of the penalty.

He holds her ankles firmly, whilst Venticello 1 thrusts the ruler under her skirts and measures her legs. Excitedly Salieri reverses his position so that he can kneel in the wing-chair, and watch. Constanze giggles delightedly, then becomes outraged – or pretends to be.

CONSTANZE   Stop it! . . . Stop that! That's quite enough of that! (*She bends down and tries to slap him.*)

VENTICELLO 1   Seventeen inches – knee to ankle!

VENTICELLO 2   Let me do it! You hold her.

CONSTANZE   That's not fair!

VENTICELLO 2   Yes, it is. You lost to me too.

CONSTANZE   It's been done now! Let me *down*!

VENTICELLO 2   Hold her, Karl.

CONSTANZE   No! . . .

Venticello 1 holds her ankles. Venticello 2 thrusts his head entirely under her skirts. She squeals.

No – stop it! . . . *No!* . . .

In the middle of this undignified scene Mozart comes rushing on – also masked.

MOZART   (*outraged*) Constanze!

They freeze. Salieri ducks back down and sits hidden in the chair.

Gentlemen, if you please.

CONSTANZE It's only a game, Wolferl! . . .

VENTICELLO 1 We meant no harm, 'pon my word.

MOZART (*stiffly*) Come down off that table please.

They hand her down.

Thank you. We'll see you later.

VENTICELLO 2 Now look, Mozart, don't be pompous –

MOZART Please excuse us now.

They go. The little man is very angry. He tears off his mask.

(*to Constanze*) Do you realize what you've done?

CONSTANZE No, what? . . . (*Flustered, she busies herself restoring the plates of sweetmeats to the table.*)

MOZART Just lost your reputation, that's all! You're now a loose girl.

CONSTANZE Don't be so stupid. (*She too removes her mask.*)

MOZART You are a married woman, for God's sake!

CONSTANZE And what of it?

MOZART A young wife does not allow her legs to be handled in public. Couldn't you at least have measured your own ugly legs?

CONSTANZE *What*? Of course they're not as good as Aloysia's! My sister had perfect legs, we all know that!

MOZART (*raising his voice*) Do you know what you've done?! . . . You've shamed me – that's all! *Shamed* me!

CONSTANZE Oh, don't be so ridiculous!

MOZART Shamed me – in front of *them*!

CONSTANZE (*suddenly furious*) You? Shamed *you*? . . . That's a laugh! If there's any shame around, lovey, it's *mine*!

MOZART What do you mean?

CONSTANZE You've only had every pupil who ever came to you.

MOZART That's not true.

CONSTANZE Every single female pupil!

MOZART Name them! *Name them!*

CONSTANZE The Aurnhammer girl! The Rumbeck girl!

38

Katherina Cavalieri – that sly little whore! *She* wasn't even your pupil – she was Salieri's. Which actually, my dear, may be why he has hundreds and you have none! He doesn't drag them into bed!

MOZART Of course he doesn't! He can't get it up, that's why! ... Have you heard his music? That's the sound of someone who *can't get it up!* At least *I* can do that!

CONSTANZE I'm sick of you!

MOZART (*shouting*) No one ever said I couldn't do *that*!

CONSTANZE (*bursting into tears*) I don't give a fart! I hate you! I hate you for ever and ever – I hate you! (*A tiny pause. She weeps.*)

MOZART (*helplessly*) Oh Stanzerl, don't cry. Please don't cry ... I can't bear it when you cry. I just didn't want you to look cheap in people's eyes, that's all. Here! (*He snatches up the ruler.*) Beat me ... Beat me ... I'm your slave. Stanzi marini. Stanzi marini bini gini. I'll just stand here like a little lamb and bear your strokes. Here. Do it ... *Batti.*

CONSTANZE No.

MOZART *Batti, batti. Mio tesoro!*

CONSTANZE No!

MOZART Stanzerly wanzerly piggly poo!

CONSTANZE Stop it.

MOZART Stanzy wanzy had a fit. Shit her stays and made them split!

She giggles despite herself.

CONSTANZE Stop it!

MOZART When they took away her skirt, Stanzy wanzy ate the dirt!

CONSTANZE Stop it now! (*She snatches the ruler and gives him a whack with it. He yowls playfully.*)

MOZART Ooooo! Oooo! Oooo! Do it again! Do it again! I cast myself at your stinking feet, Madonna!

He does so. She whacks him some more as he crouches, but always lightly, scarcely looking at him, divided between tears and laughter. Mozart drums his feet with pleasure.

MOZART Ow! Ow! Ow!

And then suddenly Salieri, unable to bear another second, cries out involuntarily.

SALIERI Ah!!!

The young couple freeze. Salieri – discovered – hastily converts his noise of disgust into a yawn, and stretches as if waking up from a nap. He peers out of the wing-chair.

Good evening.

CONSTANZE (*embarrassed*) Excellency . . .

MOZART How long have you been there?

SALIERI I was asleep until a second ago. Are you two quarrelling?

MOZART No, of course not.

CONSTANZE Yes, we are. He's been very irritating.

SALIERI (*rising*) Caro Herr, tonight is the time for New Year resolutions. Irritating lovely ladies cannot surely be one of yours. May I suggest you bring us each a *sorbetto* from the dining-room?

MOZART But why don't we all go to the table?

CONSTANZE Herr Salieri is quite right. Bring them here – it'll be your punishment.

MOZART Stanzi!

SALIERI Come now, I can keep your wife company. There cannot be a better peace offering than a *sorbetto* of aniseed.

CONSTANZE I prefer tangerine.

SALIERI Very well, tangerine. (*Greedily*) But if you could possibly manage aniseed for me, I'd be deeply obliged . . . So the New Year can begin coolly for all three of us.

A pause. Mozart hesitates – and then bows.

MOZART I'm honoured, Signore, of course. And then I'll play you at billiards. What do you say?

SALIERI   I'm afraid I don't play.

MOZART   (*with surprise*) You don't?

CONSTANZE   Wolferl would rather play at billiards than anything. He's very good at it.

MOZART   I'm the best! I may nod occasionally at composing, but at billiards – never!

SALIERI   A virtuoso of the cue.

MOZART   Exactly! It's a virtuoso's game! . . . (*He snatches up the ruler and treats it as if it were a cue.*) I think I shall write a Grand Fantasia for Billiard Balls! Trills. Aciaccaturas! Whole arpeggios in ivory! Then I'll play it myself in public! . . . It'll have to be *me* because none of those Italian charlatans like Clementi will be able to get his fingers round the cue! *Scusate*, Signore!

He gives a swanky flourish of the hand and struts off.

CONSTANZE   He's a love, really

SALIERI   And lucky, too, in you. You are, if I may say so, an astonishing creature.

CONSTANZE   Me? . . . Ta very much.

SALIERI   On the other hand, your husband does not appear to be so thriving.

CONSTANZE   (*seizing her opportunity*) We're desperate, sir.

SALIERI   What?

CONSTANZE   We've no money and no prospects of any. That's the truth.

SALIERI   I don't understand. He gives many public concerts.

CONSTANZE   They don't pay enough. What he needs is pupils. Illustrious pupils. His father calls us spendthrifts, but that's unfair. I manage as well as anyone could. There's simply not enough. Don't tell him I talked to you, please.

SALIERI   (*intimately*) This is solely between us. How can I help?

CONSTANZE   My husband needs security, sir. If only he could find regular employment, everything would be all right. Is there nothing at Court?

41

SALIERI Not at the moment.

CONSTANZE (*harder*) The Princess Elizabeth needs a tutor.

SALIERI Really? I hadn't heard.

CONSTANZE One word from you and the post would be his. Other pupils would follow at once.

SALIERI (*looking off*) He's coming back.

CONSTANZE Please ... please, Excellency. You can't imagine what a difference it would make.

SALIERI We can't speak of it now.

CONSTANZE When then? Oh, please!

SALIERI Can you come and see me tomorrow? Alone?

CONSTANZE I can't do that.

SALIERI I'm a married man.

CONSTANZE All the same.

SALIERI When does he work?

CONSTANZE Afternoons.

SALIERI Then come at three.

CONSTANZE I can't possibly!

SALIERI Yes or no? In his interests?

A pause. She hesitates – opens her mouth – then smiles and abruptly runs off.

(*to Audience*) So I'd done it. Spoken aloud. Invited her! What of that vow made in Church? Fidelity ... virtue ... all of that? ... What did she think of me – this careful Italian? Sincere friend or hopeful seducer? ... Would she come? ... I had no idea!

Servants remove the Waldstädten furniture. Others replace it with two small gilded chairs, centre, quite close together. Others again surreptitiously bring in the old dressing-gown which Salieri discarded earlier, placing them on the fortepiano.

*　　*　　*　　*

Salieri's salon

On the curtains are thrown again projections of long windows.

SALIERI   If she did, how would I behave? I had no idea of that either . . . Next afternoon I waited in a fever! Was I actually going to seduce a young wife of two months' standing . . . Part of me – much of me – wanted it, badly. Badly. Yes, badly was the word! . . .

The clock strikes three. On the first stroke the bell sounds. He rises excitedly.

There she was! On the stroke! She'd come . . . She'd *come*!

Enter from the right the Cook, still as fat, but forty years younger. He proudly carries a plate piled with brandied chestnuts. Salieri takes them from him nervously, nodding with approval, and sets them on the table.

SALIERI   (*to the Cook*) Grazie. Grazie tanti . . . Via, via, via!

The Cook bows as Salieri dismisses him, and goes out the same way, smirking suggestively. The Valet comes in from the left, – he is also forty years younger – and behind him Constanze, wearing a pretty hat and carrying a portfolio.

Signora!

CONSTANZE   (*curtseying*) Excellency.

SALIERI   Benvenuta. (*To Valet in dismissal*) Grazie.

The Valet goes.

Well. You have come.

CONSTANZE   I should not have done. My husband would be frantic if he knew. He's a very jealous man.

SALIERI   Are you a jealous woman?

CONSTANZE   Why do you ask?

SALIERI   It's not a passion I understand . . . You're looking even prettier than you were last night, if I may say so.

CONSTANZE   Ta very much! . . . I brought you some manuscripts by Wolfgang. When you see them you'll understand how right he is for a Royal Appointment. Will you look at them, please, while I wait?

SALIERI   You mean now?

CONSTANZE   Yes, I have to take them back with me. He'll miss

43

them otherwise. He doesn't make copies. These are all the originals.

SALIERI Sit down. Let me offer you something special.

CONSTANZE (*sitting*) What's that?

SALIERI (*producing the box*) *Capezzoli di Venere.* Nipples of Venus. Roman chestnuts in brandied sugar.

CONSTANZE No, thank you.

SALIERI Do try. They were made especially for you.

CONSTANZE Me?

SALIERI Yes. They're quite rare.

CONSTANZE Well then, I'd better hadn't I? Just one . . . Ta very much. (*She takes one and puts it in her mouth. The taste amazes her.*) Oh! . . . Oh! . . . Oh! . . . They're *delish!*

SALIERI (*lustfully watching her eat*) Aren't they?

CONSTANZE Mmmmm!

SALIERI Have another.

CONSTANZE (*taking two more*) I couldn't possibly.

Carefully he moves round behind her, and seats himself on the chair next to her.

SALIERI I think you're the most generous girl in the world.

CONSTANZE Generous?

SALIERI It's my word for you. I thought last night that Constanze is altogether too stiff a name for that girl. I shall rechristen her 'Generosa'. *La Generosa.* Then I'll write a glorious song for her under that title and she'll sing it, just for me.

CONSTANZE (*smiling*) I am much out of practice, sir.

SALIERI *La Generosa.* (*He leans a little towards her.*) Don't tell me it's going to prove inaccurate, my name for you.

CONSTANZE (*coolly*) What name do you give your wife, Excellency?

SALIERI (*equally coolly*) I'm not an Excellency, and I call my wife Signora Salieri. If I named her anything else it would be *La Statua.* She's a very upright lady.

CONSTANZE Is she here now? I'd like to meet her.

44

SALIERI   Alas, no. At the moment she's visiting her mother in Verona.

She starts very slightly out of her chair. Salieri gently restrains her.

Constanze: tomorrow evening I dine with the Emperor. One word from me recommending your husband as tutor to the Princess Elizabeth, and that invaluable post is his. Believe me, when I speak to His Majesty in matters musical, no one contradicts me.

CONSTANZE   I believe you.

SALIERI   *Bene. (Still sitting, he takes his mouchoir and delicately wipes her mouth with it.)* Surely service of that sort deserves a little recompense in return?

CONSTANZE   How little?

Slight pause.

SALIERI   The size of a kiss.

Slight pause.

CONSTANZE   Just one?

Slight pause.

SALIERI   If one seems fair to you.

She looks at him – then kisses him lightly on the mouth. Longer pause.

Does it?

She gives him a longer kiss. He makes to touch her with his hand. She breaks off.

CONSTANZE   I fancy that's fairness enough.

Pause.

SALIERI   *(carefully)* A pity . . . It's somewhat small pay, to secure a post every musician in Vienna is hoping for.

CONSTANZE   What do you mean?

SALIERI   Is it not clear?

CONSTANZE   No. Not at all.
SALIERI   Another pity ... A thousand pities.

Pause.

CONSTANZE   I don't believe it ... I just don't believe it!
SALIERI   What?
CONSTANZE   What you've just said.
SALIERI   (*hastily*) I said nothing! What did I say?

Constanze gets up and Salieri rises in panic.

CONSTANZE   Oh, I'm going! ... I'm getting out of this!
SALIERI   Constanze ...
CONSTANZE   Let me pass, please.
SALIERI   Constanze, listen to me! I'm a clumsy man. You think me sophisticated – I'm not at all. Take a true look. I've no cunning. I live on ink and sweetmeats. I never see women at all ... When I met you last night, I envied Mozart from the depths of my soul. Out of that envy came stupid thoughts. For one silly second I dared imagine that – out of the vast store you obviously possess – you might spare me one coin of tenderness your rich husband does not need – and inspire me also.

Pause. She laughs.

I amuse.
CONSTANZE   Mozart was right. You're wicked.
SALIERI   He said that?
CONSTANZE   'All wops are performers,' he said. 'Be very careful with that one.' Meaning you. He was being comic of course.
SALIERI   Yes.

Abruptly he turns his back on her.

CONSTANZE   But not that comic, actually. I mean you're acting a pretty obvious role, aren't you, dear? A small town boy, and all the time as clever as cutlets! ... (*Mock tender*) Ah! – you are sulking? *Are* you? ... When Mozart sulks I smack his botty. He rather likes it. Do you want me to scold you a bit and smack your botty too? (*She hits him lightly with the portfolio. He turns in a fury.*)

SALIERI How dare you?! .... *You silly, common girl!*

A dreadful silence.

(*icy*) Forgive me. Let us confine our talk to your husband. He is a brilliant keyboard player, no question. However, the Princess Elizabeth also requires a tutor in vocal music. I am not convinced he is the man for that. I would like to look at the pieces you've brought, and decide if he is mature enough. I will study them overnight – and you will study my proposal. Not to be vague: that is the price. (*He extends his hand for the portfolio, and she surrenders it.*) Good afternoon.

He turns from her and places it on a chair. She lingers – tries to speak – cannot – and goes out quickly.

*   *   *   *

The same

Salieri turns in a ferment to the Audience.

SALIERI Fiasco! .... Fiasco! .... The sordidness of it! The sheer sweating sordidness! .... Worse than if I'd actually done it! .... To be that much in sin and feel so *ridiculous* as well! There was no excuse. If now my music was rejected by God forever, it was my fault, mine alone. Would she return tomorrow? Never. And if she did, what then? What would I do? .... Apologise profoundly – or try again? ... (*Crying out*) *Nobile, nobile Salieri!* .... What had he done to me – this Mozart! Before he came did I behave like this? Did I? Toy with adultery? Blackmail women? Twist myself into cruelties? It was all going – slipping – growing *rotten* – because of *him*!

He moves upstage in a fever – reaches out to take the portfolio on the chair – but as if fearful of what he might find inside it he withdraws his hand and sits instead. A pause. He contemplates the music lying there as if it were a great confection he is dying to eat, but dare not. Then suddenly he snatches at it – tears the ribbon – opens the case and stares greedily at the manuscripts within.

Music sounds instantly, faintly, in the theatre, as his eye falls on the first page. It is the opening of the Twenty-ninth Symphony, in A Major. Over the music, reading it.

She had said that these were his original scores. First and only drafts of the music. Yet they looked like fair copies. They showed no corrections of any kind.

He looks up from the manuscript at the Audience: the music abruptly stops.

It was puzzling – then suddenly alarming. What was evident was that Mozart was simply transcribing music –

He resumes looking at the music. Immediately the Sinfonia Concertante for Violin and Viola sounds faintly.

– completely finished in his head. And finished as most music is never finished.

He looks up again: the music breaks off.

Displace one note and there would be diminishment. Displace one phrase and the structure would fall.

He resumes reading, and the music also resumes: a ravishing phrase from the slow movement of the Concerto for Flute and Harp.

Here again – only now in abundance – were the same sounds I'd heard in the library. The same crushed harmonies – glancing collisions – agonizing delights.

And he looks up: again the music stops.

The truth was clear. That Serenade had been no accident.

Very low, in the theatre, a faint thundery sound is heard accumulating, like a distant sea.

I was staring through the cage of those meticulous ink strokes

48

at an Absolute Beauty!

And out of the thundery roar writhes and rises the clear sound of a Soprano, singing the Kyrie from the C Minor Mass. The accretion of noise around her voice falls away – it is suddenly clear and bright – then clearer and brighter. The light grows bright: too bright: burning white, then scalding white! Salieri rises in the downpour of it, and in the flood of the music which is growing ever louder – filling the theatre – as the Soprano yields to the full Chorus, fortissimo, singing its massive counterpoint.

This is by far the loudest sound the Audience has yet heard. Salieri staggers towards us, holding the manuscripts in his hand, like a man caught in a tumbling and violent sea.

Finally the drums crash in below: Salieri drops the portfolio of manuscripts – and falls senseless to the ground. At the same second the music explodes into a long, echoing, distorted boom, signifying some dreadful annihilation.

The sound remains suspended over the prone figure in a menacing continuum – no longer music at all. Then it dies away, and there is only silence.

The light fades again.

A long pause.

Salieri is quite still, his head by the pile of manuscripts.

Finally the clock sounds: nine times. Salieri stirs as it does. Slowly he raises his head and looks up. And now – quietly at first – he addresses his God.

SALIERI   *Capisco!* I know my fate. Now for the first time I feel my emptiness as Adam felt his nakedness... (*Slowly he rises to his feet.*) Tonight at an inn somewhere in this city stands a giggling child who can put on paper, without actually setting down his billiard cue, casual notes which turn my most considered ones into lifeless scratches. *Grazie*, Signore! You gave me the desire to serve you – which most men do not have – then saw to it the service was shameful in the ears of the server. *Grazie!* You gave me the desire to praise you – which most do not feel – then made me mute. *Grazie tanti!* You put into me perception of the Incomparable – which most men

49

never know! – then ensured that I would know myself forever mediocre. *(His voice gains power.)* Why? ... What is my fault? ... Until this day I have pursued virtue with rigour. I have laboured long hours to relieve my fellow men. I have worked and worked the talent you allowed me. *(Calling up)* You know *how hard I've worked!* – solely that in the end, in the practice of the art which alone makes the world comprehensible to me, I might hear Your Voice! And now I do hear it – and it says only one name: MOZART! ... Spiteful, sniggering, conceited, infantine Mozart! – who has never worked one minute to help another man! – shit-talking Mozart with his botty-smacking wife! – *him* you have chosen to be your sole conduct! And *my* only reward – my sublime privilege – is to be the sole man alive in this time who shall clearly recognize your Incarnation! *(Savagely)* Grazie e grazie ancora! *(Pause)* So be it! From this time we are enemies, You and I! I'll not accept it from You – *Do you hear?* ... They say God is not mocked. I tell you, *Man* is not mocked! ... *I* am not mocked! ... They say the spirit bloweth where it listeth: I tell you NO! It must list to virtue or not blow at all! *(Yelling)* Dio Ingiusto! – You are the Enemy! I name Thee now – *Nemico Eterno!* And this I swear. To my last breath I shall *block* you on earth, as far as I am able! *(He glares up at God. To Audience)* What use, after all, is Man, if not to teach God His lessons? *(Pause. Suddenly he speaks again to us in the voice of an old man.)* And now –

He slips off his powdered wig, crosses to the fortepiano and takes from its lid the old dressing-gown and shawl which he discarded when he conducted us back to the eighteenth century. These he slips on over his court coat. It is again 1823.

before I tell you what happened next – God's answer to me – and indeed Constanze's – and all the horrors that followed – let me stop. The bladder, being a human appendage, is not something you ghosts need concern yourselves with yet. I being alive, though barely, am at its constant call. It is now one hour before dawn – when I must dismiss us both. When

I return I'll tell you about the war I fought with God through his preferred Creature – Mozart, named *Amadeus*. In the waging of which, of course, the Creature had to be destroyed.

He bows to the Audience with malignant slyness – snatches a pastry from the stand – and leaves the stage, chewing at it voraciously. The manuscripts lie where he spilled them in his fall.

The lights in the theatre come up as he goes.

END OF ACT ONE

Act Two

Salieri's salon

The lights go down in the theatre as Salieri returns.

SALIERI   I have been listening to the cats in the courtyard. They are all singing Rossini. It is obvious that cats have declined as badly as composers. Domenico Scarlatti owned one which would actually stroll across the keyboard and pick out passable subjects for fugue. But that was a Spanish cat of the Enlightenment. It appreciated counterpoint. Nowadays all cats appreciate is coloratura. Like the rest of the public.

He comes downstage and addresses the Audience directly.

This is now the very last hour of my life. You must understand me. Not forgive. I do not seek forgiveness. I was a good man, as the world calls good. *What use was it to me?* Goodness could not make me a good composer. Was Mozart good? . . . Goodness is nothing in the furnace of art.

Pause.

On that dreadful Night of the Manuscripts my life acquired a terrible and thrilling purpose. The blocking of God in one of his purest manifestations. I had the power. God needed Mozart to let himself into the world. And Mozart needed *me* to get him worldly advancement. So it would be a battle to the end – and Mozart was the battleground.

Pause.

One thing I knew of Him. God was a cunning Enemy. Witness the fact that in blocking Him in the world I was also given the satisfaction of obstructing a disliked human rival. I wonder which of you will refuse that chance if it is offered.

He regards the Audience maliciously, taking off his dressing gown and shawl.

I felt the danger at once, as soon as I'd uttered my challenge.
How would He answer? Would He strike me dead for my
impiety? Don't laugh. I was not a sophisticate of the salons.
I was a small-town Catholic, full of dread!

*He puts on his powdered wig, and speaks again in his younger voice.
We are back in the eighteenth century.*

The first thing that happened – suddenly Constanze was
back! At ten o'clock at night!

The doorbell sounds. Constanze comes in followed by a helpless Valet.

(*In surprise*) Signora!

CONSTANZE (*stiffly*) My husband is at a soirée of Baron Van
Swieten. A concert of Sebastian Bach. He didn't think I
would enjoy it.

SALIERI I see. (*Curtly, to the goggling Valet*) I'll ring if we require
anything. Thank you.

The Valet goes out. Slight pause.

CONSTANZE (*flatly*) Where do we go, then?

SALIERI What?

CONSTANZE Do we do it in here? . . . Why not?

She sits, still wearing her hat, in one of the little gilded upright chairs.
*Deliberately she loosens the strings of her bodice, so that one can just
see the tops of her breasts, hitches up her silk skirts above the knees, so
that one can also just see the flesh above the tops of the stockings, spreads
her legs and regards him with an open stare.*

(*Speaking softly*) Well? . . . Let's get on with it.

For a second Salieri returns the stare, then looks suddenly away.

SALIERI (*stiffly*) Your manuscripts are there. Please take them
and go. Now. At once.

Pause.

CONSTANZE You shit.

53

She jumps up and snatches the portfolio.

SALIERI *Via! Don't return!*
CONSTANZE You rotten shit!

Suddenly she runs at him – trying furiously to hit at his face. He grabs her arms, shakes her violently, and hurls her on the floor.

SALIERI *Via!*

She freezes, staring up at him in hate.

(*Calling to Audience*) You see how it was! I would have liked her – oh yes, just then more than ever! But now I wanted nothing petty! . . . My quarrel wasn't with Mozart – it was through him! Through him to God who loved him so. (*Scornfully*) Amadeus! . . . Amadeus! . . .

Constanze picks herself up and runs from the room.
    Pause. He calms himself, going to the table and selecting a 'Nipple of Venus' to eat.

The next day, when Katherina Cavalieri came for her lesson, I made the same halting speech about 'coins of tenderness' – and I dubbed the girl *la Generosa*. I regret that my invention in love, as in art, has always been limited. Fortunately Katherina found it sufficient. She consumed twenty 'Nipples of Venus' – kissed me with brandied breath – and slipped easily into my bed.

Katherina comes in languidly, half-dressed, as if from his bedroom. He embraces her, and helps slyly to adjust her peignoir.

She remained there as my mistress for many years behind my good wife's back – and I soon erased in sweat the sense of his little body, the Creature's, preceding me.

The girl gives him a radiant smile, and ambles off.

So much for my vow of sexual virtue. (*Slight pause.*) The same evening I went to the Palace and resigned from all my committees to help the lot of poor musicians. So much for my vow of social virtue.

Light change.

Then I went to the Emperor and recommended a man of no talent whatever to instruct the Princess Elizabeth.

*　　*　　*　　*

The Palace of Schönbrunn

The Emperor stands before the vast fireplace, between the golden mirrors.

JOSEPH Herr Sommer. A dull man, surely? What of Mozart?

SALIERI Majesty, I cannot with a clear conscience recommend Mozart to teach Royalty. One hears too many stories.

JOSEPH They may be just gossip.

SALIERI One of them I regret relates to a protégée of my own. A very young singer.

JOSEPH *Charmant!*

SALIERI Not pleasant, Majesty, but true.

JOSEPH I see ... Let it be Herr Sommer, then. (*He walks down on to the main stage.*) I daresay he can't do much harm. To be frank, no one can do much harm musically to the Princess Elizabeth. (*He strolls away.*)

Salieri goes. Mozart enters from the other side, downstage. He wears a more natural-looking wig from now on: one indeed intended to represent his own hair of light chestnut, full and gathered at the back with ribbon.

SALIERI (*To Audience*) Mozart certainly did not suspect me. The Emperor announced the appointment in his usual way –

JOSEPH (*pausing*) Well, there it is. (*Joseph goes off.*)

SALIERI – and I commiserated with the loser.

Mozart turns and stares bleakly out front. Salieri shakes his hand.

MOZART (*bitterly*) It's my own fault. My father always writes I should be more obedient. *Know my place!* ... He'll send me sixteen lectures when he hears of this!

ACT TWO

Mozart goes slowly up to the fortepiano. Lights lower.

SALIERI   (*to Audience, watching him*) It was a most serious loss as far as Mozart was concerned.

*   *   *   *

Vienna, and glimpses of opera houses

The Venticelli glide on.

VENTICELLO 1   His list of pupils hardly moves.
VENTICELLO 2   Six at most.
VENTICELLO 1   And now a child to keep!
VENTICELLO 2   A boy.
SALIERI   Poor fellow. (*To Audience*) I, by contrast, prospered. This is the extraordinary truth. If I had expected anger from God – none came. *None!* . . . Instead – incredibly – in eighty-four and eighty-five I came to be regarded as infinitely the superior composer. And this despite the fact that these were the two years in which Mozart wrote his best keyboard concerti and his string quartets.

The Venticelli stand on either side of Salieri. Mozart sits at the fortepiano.

VENTICELLO 1   Haydn calls the quartets unsurpassed.
SALIERI   They were – but no one heard them.
VENTICELLO 2   Van Swieten calls the concerti sublime.
SALIERI   They were, but no one noticed.

Mozart plays and conducts from the keyboard. Faintly we hear the Rondo from the Piano Concerto in A Major, K.488.

(*Over this*) The Viennese greeted each unique concerto with the squeals of pleasure they usually reserved for a new style of bonnet. Each was played once – then totally forgotten! . . . I alone was empowered to recognize them fully for what they were: the most perfect things made by man in the whole of the eighteenth century. By contrast, my operas were played everywhere and saluted by everyone! I composed my *Semiramide* for Munich.

VENTICELLO 1   Rapturously received!
VENTICELLO 2   People *faint* with pleasure!

In the Light Box is seen the interior of a brilliantly coloured Opera House, and an Audience standing up applauding vigorously. Salieri, flanked by the Venticelli, turns upstage and bows to it. The concerto can scarcely be heard through the din.

SALIERI   I wrote a comic opera for Vienna. *La Grotta di Trofonio*.
VENTICELLO 1   The talk of the city!
VENTICELLO 2   The cafés are buzzing!

Another Opera House interior is lit up. Another Audience claps vigorously. Again Salieri bows to it.

SALIERI   *(to Audience)* I finally finished my tragic opera *Danaius*, and produced it in Paris.
VENTICELLO 1   Stupendous reception!
VENTICELLO 2   The plaudits shake the roof!
VENTICELLO 1   Your name sounds throughout the Empire!
VENTICELLO 2   Throughout all Europe!

Yet another Opera House and another excited Audience. Salieri bows a third time. Even the Venticelli now applaud him. The concerto stops. Mozart rises from the keyboard and, whilst Salieri speaks, crosses directly through the scene and leaves the stage.

SALIERI   *(to Audience)* It was incomprehensible. Almost as if I were being pushed deliberately from triumph to triumph!...
I filled my head with golden opinions – yes, and this house with golden furniture!

*   *   *   *

Salieri's salon

The stage turns gold.
    Servants come on carrying golden chairs upholstered in golden brocade. They place these all over the wooden floor.

The Valet appears – a little older – divests Salieri of his sky-blue coat and clothes him instead in a frock-coat of gold satin.

The Cook – also of course a little older – brings in a golden cake-stand piled with more elaborate cakes.

SALIERI My own taste was for plain things – but I *denied* it! . . . I grew confident. I grew resplendent. I gave salons and soirées, and worshipped the season round at the altar of sophistication!

He sits at ease in his salon. The Venticelli sit with him, one on either side.

VENTICELLO 1 Mozart heard your comedy last night.

VENTICELLO 2 He spoke of it to the Princess Lichnowsky.

VENTICELLO 1 He said you should be made to clean up your own mess.

SALIERI *(taking snuff) Really?* What charmers these Salzburgers are!

VENTICELLO 2 People are outraged by him.

VENTICELLO 1 He empties drawing-rooms. Now Van Swieten is angry with him.

SALIERI Lord Fugue? I thought he was the Baron's little pet.

VENTICELLO 2 Mozart has asked leave to write an Italian opera.

SALIERI *(briskly aside to Audience) Italian opera! Threat! My kingdom!*

VENTICELLO 1 And the Baron is scandalized.

SALIERI But why? What's the theme of it?

Van Swieten comes on quickly from upstage.

VAN SWIETEN Figaro! . . . *The Marriage of Figaro!* That disgraceful play of Beaumarchais!

At a discreet sign of dismissal from Salieri, the Venticelli slip away. Van Swieten joins Salieri, and sits on one of the gold chairs.

(*To Salieri*) That's all he can find to waste his talent on: a vulgar farce! When I reproved him, he said I reminded him of his father! Noblemen lusting after chambermaids! Their wives dressing up in stupid disguises anyone could penetrate in a second! . . . Why set such rubbish to music?

Mozart enters quickly from upstage, accompanied by Strack. They join Salieri and Van Swieten.

MOZART   Because I want to do a piece about real people, Baron! And I want to set it in a real place! A *boudoir*! – because that to me is the most exciting place on earth! Underclothes on the floor! Sheets still warm from a woman's body! Even a pisspot brimming under the bed!

VAN SWIETEN   (*outraged*) Mozart!

MOZART   I want life, Baron. Not boring legends!

STRACK   Herr Salieri's recent *Danaius* was a legend and that did not bore the French.

MOZART   It is impossible to bore the French – except with real life!

VAN SWIETEN   I had assumed, now that you had joined our Brotherhood of Masons, you would choose more elevated themes.

MOZART   (*impatiently*) Oh elevated! Elevated! ... The only thing a man should elevate is his doodle.

VAN SWIETEN   You are provoking, sir! Has everything to be a joke with you?

MOZART   (*desperate*) Excuse language, Baron, but really! ... How can we go on forever with these gods and heroes?

VAN SWIETEN   (*passionately*) Because they *go* on forever – that's why! They represent the eternal in us. Opera is here to ennoble us, Mozart – you and me just as well as the Emperor. It is an aggrandizing art! It celebrates the eternal in Man and ignores the ephemeral. The goddess in Woman and not the laundress.

STRACK   Well said, sir. Exactly!

MOZART   (*imitating his drawl*) Oh well said, yes, well said! Exactly! (*To all of them*) I don't understand you! You're all up on perches, but it doesn't hide your arseholes! You don't give a shit about gods and heroes! If you are honest – each one of you – which of you isn't more at home with his hairdresser than Hercules? Or Horatius? (*To Salieri*) Or your stupid

59

Danaius, come to that! Or mine – *mine! Mitridate, King of Pontus! Idomeneo, King of Crete!* All those anguished antiques! They're all bores! Bores, bores, bores! (*Suddenly he springs up and jumps on to a chair, like an orator. Declaring it.*) All serious operas written this century are boring!

They turn and look at him in shocked amazement. A pause. He gives his little giggle, and then jumps up and down on the chair . . .

Look at us! Four gaping mouths. What a perfect quartet! I'd love to write it – just this second of time, this *now*, as you are! Herr Chamberlain thinking 'Impertinent Mozart: I must speak to the Emperor at once!' Herr Prefect thinking 'Ignorant Mozart: debasing opera with his vulgarity!' Herr Court Composer thinking 'German Mozart: what can he finally know about music?' And Herr Mozart himself, in the middle, thinking 'I'm just a good fellow. Why do they all disapprove of me?' (*Excitedly, to Van Swieten*) That's why opera is important, Baron. Because it's realer than any play! A dramatic poet would have to put all those thoughts down one after another to represent this second of time. The composer can put them all down at once – and still make us hear each one of them. Astonishing device: a vocal quartet! (*More and more excited*) . . . I tell you I want to write a finale lasting half an hour! A quartet becoming a quintet becoming a sextet. On and on, wider and wider – all sounds multiplying and rising together – and the together making a sound entirely new! . . . I bet you that's how God hears the world. Millions of sounds ascending at once and mixing in His ear to become an unending music, unimaginable to us! (*To Salieri*) That's our job! That's our job, we composers: combining the inner minds of him and him and him, and her and her – the thoughts of chambermaids and Court Composers – and turn the audience into God.

Pause. Salieri stares at him fascinated. Embarrassed, Mozart blows a raspberry and giggles.

I'm sorry. I talk nonsense all day: it's incurable – ask Stanzerl. (*To Van Swieten*) My tongue is stupid. My heart isn't.

VAN SWIETEN   No. You're a good fellow under all your nonsense: I know that. He'll make a fine new Brother Mason, won't he, Salieri?

SALIERI   Better than I, Baron.

VAN SWIETEN   Just try, my friend, to be more serious with your gifts.

He smiles, presses Mozart's hand, and goes. Salieri rises.

SALIERI   *Buona fortuna*, Mozart.

MOZART   *Grazie*, Signore. (*Rounding on Strack*) Stop frowning, Herr Chamberlain. I'm a jackass. It's easy to be friends with a jackass: just shake his 'hoof'.

He forms his hand into a 'hoof'. Warily Strack takes it – then springs back as Mozart brays loudly like a donkey.

MOZART   *Hee-haw!* . . . Tell the Emperor the opera's finished.

STRACK   Finished?

MOZART   Right here in my noddle. The rest's just scribbling. Goodbye.

STRACK   Good-day to you.

MOZART   He's going to be proud of me. You'll see. (*He gives his flourish of the hand and goes out, delighted with himself.*)

STRACK   That young man really is . . .

SALIERI   (*blandly*) Very lively.

STRACK   (*exploding*) Intolerable! . . . *Intolerable*!

Strack freezes in a posture of indignation.

SALIERI   (*to Audience*) How could I stop it? . . . How could I block this opera of Figaro? . . . Incredible to hear, within six weeks! . . .

Rosenberg bustles in.

ROSENBERG   Figaro is complete! The first performance will be on May the first!

SALIERI   So soon?

ROSENBERG   There's no way we can stop it!

A slight pause.

SALIERI   (*slyly*) I have an idea. *Una piccola idea!*

ROSENBERG   What?

SALIERI   *Mi ha detto che c'è un balletto nel terzo atto?*

ROSENBERG   (*puzzled*) *Sí.*

STRACK   What does he say?

SALIERI   *E dimmi – non è vero che l'Imperatore ha proibito il balletto nelle sue opere?*

ROSENBERG   (*realizing*) *Uno balletto* . . . Ah!

SALIERI   *Precisamente.*

ROSENBERG   *Oh, capisco! Ma che meraviglia! Perfetto!* (*He laughs in delight.*) *Veramente ingegnoso!*

STRACK   (*irritated*) What is it? What is he suggesting?

SALIERI   See him at the theatre.

ROSENBERG   Of course. Immediately. I'd forgotten. You are brilliant, Court Composer.

SALIERI   I? . . . I have said nothing. (*He moves away upstage.*)

The dim light begins to change, dimming down.

STRACK   (*very cross*) I must tell you that I resent this extremely. Mozart is right in some things. There is far too much Italian *chittero-chattero* at this Court! Now please to inform me at once, what was just said?

ROSENBERG   (*lightly*) *Pazienza*, my dear Chamberlain. *Pazienza.* Just wait and see!

From upstage Salieri beckons to Strack. Baffled and cross, the Chamberlain joins him. They watch together, unseen. The light dims further.

*   *   *   *

An unlit theatre

In the background a projection of lamps glowing faintly in the darkened auditorium. Rosenberg sits on one of the gold chairs, centre.

Mozart comes in quickly from the left, wearing another bright coat, and carrying the score of Figaro. *He crosses to the fortepiano.*

ROSENBERG Mozart . . . *Mozart!*

MOZART Yes, Herr Director.

ROSENBERG *(agreeably)* A word with you, please. Right away.

MOZART Certainly. What is it?

ROSENBERG I would like to see your score of *Figaro*.

MOZART Oh yes. Why?

ROSENBERG Just bring it here to me. *(Unmoving)* Into my hand, please.

Mozart hands it to him puzzled. Rosenberg turns the pages.

Now tell me: did you not know that His Majesty has expressly forbidden ballet in his operas?

MOZART Ballet?

ROSENBERG Such as occurs in your third act.

MOZART That is not a ballet, Herr Director. That is a dance at Figaro's wedding.

ROSENBERG Exactly. A dance.

MOZART *(trying to control himself)* But, the Emperor doesn't mean to prohibit dancing when it's part of the story. He made that law to prevent *insertions* of stupid ballet like in French operas, and quite right too.

ROSENBERG *(raising his voice)* It is not for you, Herr Mozart, to interpret the Emperor's edicts. Merely to obey them. *(He seizes the offending pages between his fingers.)*

MOZART What are you doing? . . . What are you doing, Excellency?

ROSENBERG Taking out what should never have been put in.

In a terrible silence Rosenberg tears out the pages, Mozart watches in disbelief. Upstage Salieri and Strack look on together from the dimness.

Now, sir, perhaps in future you will obey Imperial commands. *(He tears out some more pages.)*

MOZART But . . . But – if all that goes – there'll be a hole right at the climax of the story!... *(Crying out suddenly)* Salieri! This is Salieri's idea!

ROSENBERG   Don't be absurd.

SALIERI   *(to Audience)* How did he think of that? Nothing I had ever done could possibly make him think of that on his own. Had God given him the idea?!

MOZART   It's a conspiracy. I can smell it. I can smell it!

ROSENBERG   Control yourself!

MOZART   *(howling) But what do you expect me to do?* The first performance is two days off!

ROSENBERG   Write it over. That's your forte, is it not? – writing at speed.

MOZART   Not when the music's *perfect*! Not when it's absolutely perfect as it is!... *(Wildly)* I shall appeal to the Emperor! I'll go to him myself! I'll hold a rehearsal especially for him.

ROSENBERG   The Emperor does not attend rehearsals.

MOZART   He'll attend this one. Make no mistake – he'll come to this one! Then he'll deal with *you*!

ROSENBERG   This issue is simple. Write your act again today – or withdraw the opera. That's final.

Pause. He hands back the mutilated score to its composer. Mozart is shaking.

MOZART   You shit-pot.

Rosenberg turns and walks imperturbably away from him.

Woppy, foppy, wet-arsed, Italian-loving, shit-pot!

Serenely, Rosenberg leaves the stage.

(Screeching after him) Count Orsini-Rosenshit!... Rosencunt! ... Rosenbugger!... I'll hold a rehearsal! You'll see! The Emperor will come! You'll see! You'll see!... *You'll see!!* *(He throws down his score in a storm of hysterical rage.)*

Upstage in the dimness Strack goes out, and Salieri ventures down towards the shrieking little man. Mozart suddenly becomes aware of him. He turns, his hand shooting out in an involuntary gesture of accusation.

(*To Salieri*) I am *forbidden*!.... I am – forbidden!.... But of course you know already!

SALIERI   (*quietly*) Know what?

Mozart flings away from him.

MOZART   (*bitterly*) No matter!

SALIERI   (*always blandly*) Mozart, permit me. If you wish, I will speak to the Emperor myself. Ask him to attend a rehearsal.

MOZART   (*amazed*) You wouldn't.

SALIERI   I cannot promise he will come – but I can try.

MOZART   Sir! –

SALIERI   Good-day. (*He puts up his hands, barring further intimacy.*)

Mozart retreats to the fortepiano.

(*to Audience*) Needless to say I did nothing whatever in the matter. Yet – to my total stupefaction –

Strack and Rosenberg hurry on downstage.

– in the middle of the last rehearsal of *Figaro* next day ...

The Emperor Joseph comes on from upstage.

JOSEPH   (*cheerfully*) Fêtes and fireworks! Fêtes and fireworks! Gentlemen, good afternoon!

*   *   *   *

The theatre

SALIERI   (*to Audience*) Entirely against his usual practice, the Emperor appeared!

Strack and Rosenberg look at each other in consternation. Joseph seats himself excitedly on one of the gold chairs, facing out front. As with the premiere of 'Seraglio' seen in Act One, he watches the Audience as if it were the opera.

JOSEPH   I can't wait for this, Mozart, I assure you! *Je prévois des merveilles!*

MOZART   (*bowing fervently*) Majesty!

The Courtiers sit also: Strack on his right-hand side, Rosenberg on his left. Salieri also sits, near the keyboard.

SALIERI   (*to Audience*) What did this mean? Was this proof God had finally decided to defend Mozart against me? Was He engaging with me at last?

Mozart passes behind Salieri.

MOZART   (*earnestly, sotto voce*) I am so grateful to you, I cannot express it!

SALIERI   (*aside, to him*) Hush. Say nothing.

Mozart goes on quickly to the fortepiano and sits at it.

(*to Audience*) One thing about the event certainly seemed more than coincidence.

Music sounds faintly: the end of the third act of Figaro, *just before the dance music starts.*

Strangely, His Majesty had arrived at precisely the moment when the dancers would have begun, (*pause*) had not they and their music been entirely cut.

The music stops abruptly.

He and all of us watched the action proceed in total silence.

Flanked by his Courtiers, the Emperor stares out front, following with his eyes what is obviously a silent pantomime. His face expresses bewilderment. Rosenberg watches his sovereign anxiously. Finally the monarch speaks.

JOSEPH   I don't understand. Is it modern?

MOZART   (*jumping up nervously from the keyboard*) No, Majesty.

JOSEPH   Then what?

MOZART   The Herr Director has removed a dance that would have occurred at this point.

JOSEPH   (*to Rosenberg*) Why was this done?

ROSENBERG It's your own regulation, Sire. No ballet in your opera.

MOZART Majesty, this is not a ballet. It is part of a wedding feast: entirely necessary for the story.

JOSEPH Well, it certainly looks very odd the way it is. I can't say I like it.

MOZART Nor do I, Majesty.

JOSEPH Do you like it, Rosenberg?

ROSENBERG It's not a question of liking, Majesty. Your own law decrees it.

JOSEPH Yes. All the same, this is nonsense. Look at them: they're like waxworks up there.

ROSENBERG Well, not exactly, Majesty.

JOSEPH I don't like waxworks.

MOZART Nor do I, Majesty.

JOSEPH Well, who would? What do you say, Salieri?

SALIERI Italians are fond of waxworks, Majesty. (*Pause*) Our religion is largely based upon them.

JOSEPH You are *cattivo* again, Court Composer.

STRACK (*intervening creamily*) Your Majesty, Count Rosenberg is very worried that if this music is put back it will create the most unfortunate precedent. One will have thereafter to endure hours of dancing in opera.

JOSEPH I think we can guard against that, you know, Chamberlain. I really think we can guard against hours of dancing. (*To Rosenberg*) Please restore Herr Mozart's music.

ROSENBERG But Majesty, I must insist –

JOSEPH (*with a touch of anger*) You will oblige me, Rosenberg! I wish to hear Mozart's music. Do you understand me?

ROSENBERG Yes, Majesty.

Mozart explodes with joy, jumps over a chair and throws himself at Joseph's feet.

MOZART Oh God, I thank your Majesty! (*He kisses the Emperor's hand extravagantly, as at their first meeting.*) Oh thank you – thank you – thank you Sire, forever!

JOSEPH (*withdrawing hand*) Yes, yes – very good. A little less enthusiasm, I beg you!

MOZART (*abashed*) Excuse me.

The Emperor rises. All follow suit.

JOSEPH Well. *There it is!*

* * * *

The first performance of Figaro

The theatre glows with light for the first performance of Figaro. *Courtiers and Citizens come in swiftly.*

The Emperor and his Court resume their seats and the others quickly take theirs. In the front row we note Katherina Cavalieri, all plumes and sequins, and Kapellmeister Bonno – older than ever. Behind them sit Constanze and the Venticelli. All of them stare out at the Audience as if it were the opera they have come to see: people of fashion down front; poorer people crowded into the Light Box upstage.

Salieri crosses as he speaks to where two chairs have been placed side by side apart from the rest, on the left, to form his box. On the chair upstage sits his good wife Teresa – more statuesque than ever.

SALIERI (*to Audience*) And so *Figaro* was produced in spite of all my efforts. I sat in my box and watched it happen. A conspicuous defeat for me. And yet I was strangely excited.

Faintly we hear Figaro singing the tune of 'Non più andrai'. The stage audience is obviously delighted: they smile out front as they watch the (invisible) action.

My March! My poor March of Welcome – now set to enchant the world forever!

It fades. Applause. The Emperor rises, and with him the audience, to denote an Intermission. Joseph greets Katherina and Bonno. Rosenberg and Strack go to Salieri's box.

ROSENBERG (*to Salieri*) Almost in your style, that last bit.

But more vulgar of course. Far more obvious than you would ever be.

STRACK (*drawling*) Exactly!

A bell rings for the end of the Intermission. The Emperor returns quickly to his seat. The audience sits. A pause. All look out front, unmoving.

SALIERI (*raptly and quietly: to Audience.*) Trembling, I heard the second act. (*Pause.*) The restored third act. (*Pause.*) The astounding fourth. What shall I say to you who will one day hear this last act for yourselves? You will – because whatever else shall pass away, this must remain.

Faintly we hear the solemn closing ensemble from Act Four of Figaro, '*Ah! Tutti contenti. Saremo cosi*'.

(*Over this*) The scene was night in a summer garden. Pinprick stars gleamed down on shaking summerhouses. Plotters glided behind pasteboard hedges. I saw a woman, dressed in her maid's clothes, hear her husband utter the first tender words he has offered her in years only because he thinks she is someone else. Could one catch a realer moment? And how except in a net of pure artifice? The disguises of opera had been invented for Mozart. (*He can barely look out at the 'stage'.*) The final reconciliation melted sight. (*Pause*) Through my tears I saw the Emperor yawn.

Joseph yawns. The music fades. There is scant applause. Joseph rises and the courtiers follow suit. Mozart bows.

JOSEPH (*coolly*) Most ingenious, Mozart. You are coming along nicely . . . I do think we must omit encores in future. It really makes things far too long. Make a note, Rosenberg.

ROSENBERG Majesty.

Mozart lowers his head, crushed.

JOSEPH Gentlemen, good night to you. Strack, attend me.

Joseph goes out, with Strack. Director Rosenberg gives Mozart one triumphant look and follows. Salieri nods to his wife who leaves with the audience. Only Constanze lingers for a second, then she too goes. A pause. Mozart and Salieri are left alone: Salieri deeply shaken by the opera, Mozart deeply upset by its reception. He crosses and sits next to Salieri.

MOZART   (*low*) Herr Salieri.

SALIERI   Yes?

MOZART   What do you think? Do you think I am coming along nicely?

SALIERI   (*moved*) I think the piece is . . . extraordinary. I think it is . . . *marvellous*. Yes.

Pause. Mozart turns to him.

MOZART   I'll tell you what it is. It's the best opera yet written. That's what it is. And only I could have done it. No one else living!

Salieri turns his head swiftly, as if he has been slapped. Mozart rises and walks away. The light changes. The Venticelli rush on. Salieri and Mozart both freeze.

VENTICELLO 1   Rosenberg is furious.

VENTICELLO 2   He'll never forgive Mozart.

VENTICELLO 1   He'll do anything to get back at him!

SALIERI   (*rising: to Audience*) So it wasn't hard to get the piece cancelled. I saw to it through the person of the resentful Director that in the entire year *Figaro* was played only *nine times*! . . . My defeat finally turned into a victory. And God's response to my challenge remained as inscrutable as ever . . . Was He taking any notice of me *at all*? . . .

Mozart breaks his freeze and comes downstage.

MOZART   *Withdrawn!* Absolutely no plans for its revival!

SALIERI   I commiserate with you, my friend. But if the public does not like one's work, one has to accept the fact gracefully. (*Aside, to Audience*) And certainly they didn't.

VENTICELLO 1   (*complaining*) It's too complicated!

VENTICELLO 2   (*complaining*) Too tiresome!

VENTICELLO 1   All those weird harmonies!

VENTICELLO 2   And never a good bang at the end of songs so you know when to clap!

The Venticelli go off.

SALIERI   (*to Audience*) Obviously I would not need to plot too hard against his operas in future. The Viennese could be relied upon to destroy those for me. I must concentrate on the man. I decided to see him as much as possible; to learn everything I could of his weaknesses.

*   *   *   *

The Waldstädten Library

Servants again bring on the wing-chair.

MOZART   I'll go to England. England loves music. That's the answer!

SALIERI   (*to Audience*) We were yet again in the library of the Baroness Waldstädten: that room fated to be the scene of ghastly encounters between us. Again, too, the compensating *crema al mascarpone.*

He sits in the chair and eats greedily.

MOZART   I was there when I was a boy. They absolutely adored me. I had more kisses than you've had cakes! . . . When I was a child, people loved me.

SALIERI   Perhaps they will again. Why don't you go to London and try?

MOZART   Because I have a wife and child and no money. I wrote to Papa to take the boy off my hands just for a few months so I could go – and he refused! . . . In the end everyone betrays you. Even the man you think loves you best . . . He's a bitter man, of course. After he'd finished showing me off around Europe he never went anywhere himself. He just stayed up in Salzburg year after year, kissing the ring of the Fartsbishop and lecturing me!... (*Confidentially*) The real thing is, you see, he's jealous. Under everything he's jealous of me! He'll never forgive me for being cleverer than he is.

He leans excitedly over Salieri's chair like a naughty child.

I'll tell you a secret. Leopold Mozart is just a jealous, dried up old turd ... And I actually detest him.

He giggles guiltily. The Venticelli appear quickly, and address Salieri, as Mozart freezes.

VENTICELLO 1   (*solemnly*) Leopold Mozart –
VENTICELLO 2   (*solemnly*) Leopold Mozart –
VENTICELLO 1 and VENTICELLO 2   *Leopold Mozart is dead!*

They go off. Mozart recoils. A long pause.

SALIERI   Do not despair. Death is inevitable, my friend.
MOZART   (*desperately*) How will I go now?
SALIERI   What do you mean?
MOZART   In the world. There's no one else. No one who understands the wickedness around. *I can't see it!* ... He watched for me all my life – and I betrayed him.
SALIERI   No!
MOZART   I talked against him.
SALIERI   No!
MOZART   (*distressed*) I married where he begged me not. I left him alone. I danced and played billiards and fooled about, and he sat by himself night after night in an empty house, and no woman to care for him ...

Salieri rises in concern.

SALIERI   Wolfgang. My dear Wolfgang. Don't accuse yourself! ... Lean upon me, if you care to ... Lean upon me.

Salieri opens his arms in a wide gesture of paternal benevolence. Mozart approaches, and is almost tempted to surrender to the embrace. But at the last moment he avoids it, and breaks away down front, to fall on his knees.

MOZART *Papa!*

SALIERI (*to Audience*) So rose the Ghost Father in *Don Giovanni*!

*   *   *   *

The two grim chords which open the Overture to 'Don Giovanni' sound through the theatre. Mozart seems to quail under them, as he stares out front. On the backdrop in the Light Box appears the silhouette of a giant black figure, in cloak and tricorne hat. It extends its arms, menacingly and engulfingly, towards its begetter.

SALIERI A Father more accusing than any in opera. So rose the figure of a Guilty Libertine, cast into Hell! . . . I looked on astounded as from his ordinary life he made his art. We were both ordinary men, he and I. Yet he from the ordinary created legends – and I from legends created only the ordinary.

The figure fades. Salieri stands over the kneeling Mozart.

Could I not have stopped my war? Shown him some pity? Oh yes, my friends, at any time – if He above had shown me one drop of it! Every day I set to work I prayed – I still prayed, you understand – 'Make this one good in my ears! Just this one! *One!*' But would He ever? . . . I heard my music calmed in convention – not one breath of spirit to lift it off the shallows. And I heard *his* –

We hear the exquisite strains of the terzetto 'Soave sia il vento' from Cosi Fan Tutte.

– the spirit singing through it unstoppable to my ears alone! I heard his comedy of the seduction of two sisters, *Cosi Fan Tutte: Thus do all women.* Aloysia and Constanze immortalized – two average girls turned into divinities: their sounds of surrender sweeter than the psalms in Heaven. (*To God, in anguish*) Grant this to me! . . . *Grant this to me!* . . . (*As 'God'*) 'No, no, no: I do not need you, Salieri! I have Mozart! Better for you to be silent!' *Hahahahaha!*

The music cuts off.

The Creature's dreadful giggle was the laughter of God. I had to end it. But how? There was only one way. *Starvation.* Starve out the God! Reduce the man to destitution.

*　　*　　*　　*

Vienna and the Palace of Schönbrunn

SALIERI　(*to Mozart*) How do you fare today?

MOZART　Badly. I have no money, and no prospect of any.

SALIERI　It would not be too hard, surely.

Lights up on the Palace of Schönbrunn. The Emperor stands in the Light Box, in his golden space.

JOSEPH　We must find him a Post.

SALIERI　(*to Audience*) One danger! The Emperor.

Salieri goes upstage to Joseph.

There's nothing available, Majesty.

JOSEPH　There's Chamber Composer now that Gluck is dead.

SALIERI　(*shocked*) Mozart to follow Gluck?

JOSEPH　I won't have him say I drove him away. You know what a tongue he has.

SALIERI　Then grant him Gluck's post, Majesty, but not his salary. That would be wrong.

JOSEPH　Gluck got two thousand florins a year. What should Mozart get?

SALIERI　Two hundred. Light payment, yes, but for light duties.

JOSEPH　Perfectly fair. I'm obliged to you, Court Composer.

SALIERI　(*bowing*) Majesty.

Lights down a little on Joseph, who still stands there. Salieri returns to Mozart.

(*To Audience*) Easily done. Like many men obsessed with being thought generous, the Emperor Joseph was quintessentially stingy.

Mozart kneels before the Emperor.

JOSEPH   Herr Mozart. *Vous nous faites honneur!* . . .

Lights. Mozart turns and walks downstage.

MOZART   It's a damned insult! Not enough to keep a mouse in cheese for a week!

SALIERI   Regard it as a token, *caro* Herr.

MOZART   When I was young they gave me snuff boxes. Now it's tokens! And for what? Pom-pom, for fireworks! Twang-twang for Contredanzes!

SALIERI   I'm sorry it's made you angry. I'd not have suggested it if I'd known you'd be distressed.

MOZART   You suggested it?

SALIERI   I regret I was not able to do more.

MOZART   Oh . . . forgive me! You're a good man! I see that now! You're a truly kind man – and I'm a monstrous fool!

He grasps Salieri's hand.

SALIERI   No, please . . .

MOZART   You make me ashamed . . . You excellent man!

SALIERI   No, no, no, no – *s'il vous plaît.* A little less enthusiasm I beg you!

Mozart laughs delightedly at this imitation of the Emperor. Salieri joins in. Mozart suddenly doubles over with stomach cramps. He groans.

   Wolfgang! What is it?

MOZART   I get cramps sometimes in my stomach.

SALIERI   I'm sorry.

MOZART   Excuse me . . . it's nothing really.

SALIERI   I will see you soon again?

MOZART   Of course.

SALIERI   Why not visit me?

MOZART   I will . . . I promise!

SALIERI   *Bene.*

MOZART   *Bene.*

SALIERI   My friend. My new friend.

Mozart giggles with pleasure and goes off. A pause.

(*To Audience*) Now if ever was the moment for God to crush me. I waited – and do you know what happened? I had just ruined Mozart's career at Court; God rewarded me by granting my dearest wish!

The Venticelli come on.

VENTICELLO 1   Kapellmeister Bonno.
VENTICELLO 2   Kapellmeister Bonno.
VENTICELLO 1 and VENTICELLO 2   *Kapellmeister Bonno is dead!*

Salieri opens his mouth in surprise.

VENTICELLO 1   You are appointed –
VENTICELLO 2   By Royal Decree –
VENTICELLO 1   To fill his place.

Lights full up on the Emperor at the back. He is flanked by Strack and Rosenberg, standing like icons as at their first appearance.

JOSEPH   (*formally as Salieri turns and bows to him*) First Royal and Imperial Kapellmeister to our Court.

The Venticelli applaud.

VENTICELLO 1   Bravo.
VENTICELLO 2   Bravo.
ROSENBERG   *Evviva*, Salieri!
STRACK   Well done, Salieri!
JOSEPH   (*warmly*) Dear Salieri – there it is!

The lights go down on Schönbrunn. In the dark the Emperor and his Court leave the stage for the last time. Salieri turns round, alarmed.

SALIERI   (*to Audience*) I was now truly alarmed. How long would I go unpunished?
VENTICELLO 1 and VENTICELLO 2   Congratulations, Sir!
VENTICELLO 1   Mozart looks appalling.

VENTICELLO 2   It must be galling of course.

VENTICELLO 1   I hear he's dosing himself constantly with medicine.

SALIERI   For what?

VENTICELLO 2   Envy, I imagine.

VENTICELLO 1   I hear there's another child on the way . . .

VENTICELLO 2   There is, I've seen the mother.

*   *   *   *

The Prater

Fresh green trees appear on the backdrop. The light changes to yellow, turning the blue surround into a rich verdant green.

Mozart and Constanze enter arm-in-arm. She is palpably pregnant and wears a poor coat and bonnet; his clothes are poorer too. Salieri promenades with the Venticelli.

SALIERI   I met him next in the Prater.

MOZART   (*to Salieri*) Congratulations, sir!

SALIERI   I thank you. And to you both! (*To Audience*) Clearly there was a change for the worse. His eyes gleamed, oddly, like a dog's when the light catches. (*To Mozart*) I hear you are not well, my friend.

He acknowledges Constanze, who curtseys to him.

MOZART   I'm not. My pains stay with me.

SALIERI   How wretched. What can they be?

MOZART   Also, I sleep badly . . . I have . . . bad dreams.

CONSTANZE   (*warningly*) Wolferl!

SALIERI   Dreams?

MOZART   Always the same one . . . A figure comes to me cloaked in grey – doing this. (*He beckons slowly.*) It has no face. Just grey – like a mask . . . (*He giggles nervously.*) What can it mean, do you think?

SALIERI   Surely you do not believe in dreams?

MOZART   No, of course not – really!

SALIERI   Surely *you* do not, Madame?

CONSTANZE   I never dream, sir. Things are unpleasant enough to me, awake.

Salieri bows.

MOZART   It's all fancy, of course!

CONSTANZE   If Wolfgang had proper work he might dream less, First Kapellmeister.

MOZART   (*embarrassed, taking her arm*) Stanzi, please! . . . Excuse us, sir. Come, dearest. We are well enough, thank you!

Husband and wife go off.

VENTICELLO 1   He's growing freakish.

VENTICELLO 2   No question.

VENTICELLO 1   Grey figures with masked faces!

SALIERI   (*looking after him*) He broods on his father too much, I fancy. Also his circumstances make him anxious.

VENTICELLO 1   They've moved house again.

VENTICELLO 2   To the Rauhensteingasse. Number nine hundred and seventy.

VENTICELLO 1   They must be desperate.

VENTICELLO 2   It's a real slum.

SALIERI   Does he earn any money at all, apart from his Post?

VENTICELLO 1   Nothing whatever.

VENTICELLO 2   I hear he's starting to beg.

VENTICELLO 1   They say he's written letters to twenty Brother Masons.

SALIERI   Really?

VENTICELLO 2   And they're giving him money.

SALIERI   (*to Audience*) Of course! They *would*! . . . I had *forgotten* the Masons! *Naturally* they would relieve him – *how stupid of me!* . . . There could be no finally starving him with the Masons there to help! As long as he asked they would keep supplying his wants . . . How could I stop it? And quickly! . . .

VENTICELLO 1   Lord Fugue is most displeased with him!

SALIERI   *Is* he?

*   *   *   *

A Masonic Lodge

A huge golden emblem descends, encrusted with Masonic symbols, enter Van Swieten. He is wearing the ritual apron over his sober clothes. At the same time Mozart enters from the left. He too wears the apron. The two men clasp hands in fraternal greeting.

VAN SWIETEN (*gravely*) This is not good, Brother. The Lodge was not created for you to beg from.

MOZART What else can I do?

VAN SWIETEN Give concerts, as you used to do.

MOZART I have no subscribers left, Baron. I am no longer fashionable.

VAN SWIETEN I am not surprised. You write tasteless comedies which give offence. I warned you, often enough.

MOZART (*humbly*) You did. I admit it. (*He holds his stomach in pain.*)

VAN SWIETEN I will send you some fugues of Bach tomorrow. You can arrange those for my Sunday concert. You shall have a small fee.

MOZART Thank you, Baron.

Van Swieten nods and goes out. Salieri steps forward. He again wears the Masonic apron.

MOZART (*shouting after Van Swieten*) I cannot live by arranging Bach!

SALIERI (*sarcastically*) A generous fellow.

MOZART All the same, I'll have to do it. If he were to turn the Lodge against me, I'd be finished. My Brother Masons virtually keep me now.

SALIERI That's fine.

MOZART Never mind. I'll manage: you'll see! Things are looking up already. I've had a marvellous proposal from Schikaneder. He's a new Member of this Lodge.

SALIERI Schikaneder? The actor?

MOZART Yes. He owns a theatre in the suburbs.

SALIERI Well, more of a music-hall, surely?

MOZART   Yes ... He wants me to write him a vaudeville –
something for ordinary German people. Isn't that a wonderful
idea? ... He's offered me half the receipts when we open.

SALIERI   Nothing in advance?

MOZART   He said he couldn't afford anything. I know it's not
much of an offer. But a popular piece about Brotherly Love
could celebrate everything we believe as Masons!

SALIERI   It certainly could! ... Why don't you put the Masons
into it?

MOZART   Into an opera? ... I couldn't!

Salieri laughs, to indicate that he was simply making a joke.

All the same – what an idea!

SALIERI   (*earnestly*) Our rituals are secret, Wolfgang.

MOZART   I needn't copy them exactly. I could adapt them a
little.

SALIERI   Well ... It would certainly be in a great cause.

MOZART   Brotherly Love!

SALIERI   Brotherly Love!

*They both turn and look solemnly at the great golden emblem hanging
at their backs.*

(*warmly*) Try it and see. Take courage, Wolfgang. It's a glorious
idea.

MOZART   It is, isn't it? It *really is*!

SALIERI   Of course say nothing till it's done.

MOZART   Not a word.

SALIERI   (*making a sign: closed fist*) Secret!

MOZART   (*making a similar sign*) Secret!

SALIERI   Good.

He steps out of the scene downstage.

(*To audience*) And if that didn't finish him off with the Masons
– nothing would!

The gold emblem withdraws. We hear the merry dance of Monastatos and the hypnotized slaves from The Magic Flute: *'Das Klinget so herrlich, Das Klinget so schön!' To the tinkling of the glockenspiel Servants bring in a long plain table loaded with manuscripts and bottles. It also bears a plain upturned stool. They place this in the wooden area head-on to the Audience. At the same time Constanze appears wearily from the back, and enters this apartment: the Rauhensteingasse. She wears a stuffed apron, indicating the advanced state of her pregnancy. Simultaneously upstage left, two other Servants have placed the little gilded table bearing a loaded cake-stand and three of the gilded chairs from Salieri's resplendent Salon. We now have in view the two contrasting apartments.*

As soon as the emblem withdraws, the Venticelli appear to Salieri.

* * * *

Mozart's apartment : Salieri's apartment

VENTICELLO 1   Mozart is delighted with himself!
VENTICELLO 2   He's writing a secret opera!
VENTICELLO 1   (*crossly*) And won't tell anyone its theme.
VENTICELLO 2   It's really too tiresome.

The Venticelli go off.

SALIERI   He told *me*. He told me everything!... Initiation ceremonies. Ceremonies with blindfolds. All rituals copied from the Masons!... He sat at home preparing his own destruction. A home where life grew daily more grim.

He goes upstage and sits on one of his gilded chairs, devouring a cake. Mozart also sits at his table, wrapped in a blanket, and starts to write music. Opposite him Constanze sits on a stool, wrapped in a shawl.

CONSTANZE   I'm cold ... I'm cold all day ... hardly surprising since we have no firewood.
MOZART   Papa was right. We end exactly as he said. Beggars.
CONSTANZE   It's all his fault.
MOZART   Papa's?
CONSTANZE   He kept you a baby all your life.

81

MOZART   I don't understand. You always loved Papa.

CONSTANZE   Did I?

MOZART   You adored him. You told me so often.

Slight pause.

CONSTANZE   (*flatly*) I hated him.

MOZART   What?

CONSTANZE   And he hated me.

MOZART   That's absurd. He loved us both very much. You're being extremely silly now.

CONSTANZE   Am I?

MOZART   (*airily*) Yes, you are, little-wife-of-my-heart!

CONSTANZE   Do you remember the fire we had last night, because it was so cold you couldn't even get the ink wet? You said, 'What a blaze' – remember? 'What a blaze! All those old papers going up!' Well, my dear, those old papers were just all your Father's letters, that's all – every one he wrote since the day we married.

MOZART   *What?*

CONSTANZE   Every one! All the letters about what a ninny I am – what a bad housekeeper I am! Every one!

MOZART   (*crying out*) Stanzi!

CONSTANZE   *Shit on him! . . . Shit on him!*

MOZART   *You bitch!*

CONSTANZE   (*savagely*) At least it kept us warm! What else will do that? Perhaps we should dance! You love to dance, Wolferl – let's dance! Dance to keep warm! (*Grandly*) Write me a contredanze, Mozart! It's your job to write dances, isn't it?

Hysterical, she starts dancing roughly round the room like a demented peasant to the tune of 'Non più andrai'.

(*Singing wildly*) Non più andrai, farfallone amoroso –
Notte e giorno d'intorno girando!

MOZART   (*shrieking*) Stop it! Stop it! (*He seizes her.*) Stanzi-marini! Marini-bini! Don't, please. Please, please, please I beg you ... Look there's a kiss! Where's it coming from? Right out of that corner! There's another one – all wet, all sloppy wet coming straight to *you*! Kiss – kiss – kiss!

She pushes him away. Constanze dances. Mozart catches her. She pushes him away.

CONSTANZE Get off!

Pause.

MOZART I'm frightened, Stanzi. Something awful's happening to me.

CONSTANZE I can't bear it. I can't bear much more of this.

MOZART And the Figure's like this now – (*Beckoning faster*) 'Here! Come here! Here!' Its face still masked – invisible! It becomes realer and realer to me!

CONSTANZE Stop it, for God's sake! ... Stop! ... It's me who's frightened ... *Me*! ... You frighten me ... If you go on like this I'll leave you. I swear it.

MOZART (*shocked*) Stanzi!

CONSTANZE I mean it ... I do ...

She puts her hand to her stomach, as if in pain.

MOZART I'm sorry ... Oh God, I'm sorry ... I'm sorry, I'm sorry, I'm sorry! ... Come here to me, little wife of my heart! Come ... Come ...

He kneels and coaxes her to him. She comes half-reluctantly, half-willingly.

Who am I? ... Quick: tell me. Hold me and tell who I am.

CONSTANZE Pussy-wussy.

MOZART Who else?

CONSTANZE Miaowy-powy.

MOZART And you're squeeky-peeky. And Stanzi-manzi. And Bini-gini!

She surrenders.

CONSTANZE   Wolfi-polfi!

MOZART   Poopy-peepee!

They giggle.

CONSTANZE   Now don't be stupid.

MOZART   (*insistent: like a child*) Come on – do it. Do it – Let's do it. 'Poppy!'

They play a private game, gradually doing it faster, on their knees.

CONSTANZE   Poppy.

MOZART   (*changing it*) Pappy.

CONSTANZE   (*copying*) Pappy.

MOZART   Pappa.

CONSTANZE   Pappa.

MOZART   Pappa-pappa!

CONSTANZE   Pappa-pappa!

MOZART   Pappa-pappa-pappa-pappa!

CONSTANZE   Pappa-pappa-pappa-pappa!

They rub noses.

TOGETHER   Pappa-pappa-pappa-pappa! Pappa-pappa-pappa-pappa!

CONSTANZE   *Ah!*

She suddenly cries out in distress, and clutches her stomach.

MOZART   Stanzi! . . . Stanzi, what is it?

The Venticelli hurry in.

VENTICELLO 1   News!

VENTICELLO 2   Suddenly!

VENTICELLO 1   She's been delivered.

VENTICELLO 2   Unexpectedly.

VENTICELLO 1   Of a boy!

VENTICELLO 2   Poor little imp.

VENTICELLO 1   To be born to that couple.

VENTICELLO 2   In that room.

VENTICELLO 1   With that money.

VENTICELLO 2   And the father a baby himself.

During the above Constanze has slowly risen, and divested herself of her stuffed apron – thereby ceasing to be pregnant. Now she turns sorrowfully and walks slowly upstage and off it.

Mozart follows her for a few steps, alarmed. He halts.

VENTICELLO 1   And now I hear –

VENTICELLO 2   Now I hear –

VENTICELLO 1   Something more has happened.

VENTICELLO 2   Even stranger.

Mozart picks up a bottle – then moves swiftly into Salieri's room.

MOZART   *(wildly)* She's gone!

SALIERI   What do you mean?

The Venticelli go off. Mozart moves up to Salieri's apartment, holding his bottle, and sits on one of the gilded chairs.

MOZART   Stanzerl's gone away! Just for a while, she says. She's taken the baby and gone to Baden. To the spa ... It will cost us the last money we have!

SALIERI   But *why*?

MOZART   She's right to go ... It's my fault ... She thinks I'm mad.

SALIERI   Surely not?

MOZART   Perhaps I am ... I think I am ... Yes ...

SALIERI   Wolfgang ...

MOZART   *(disturbed)* Let me tell you! Last night I saw the Figure again – the figure in my dreams. Only this time I was *awake*! *(Very disturbed)* It stood before my table, all in grey, its face still grey, still masked. And this time it spoke to me! 'Wolfgang Mozart – you must write now a Requiem Mass. Take up your pen and begin!'

SALIERI   A Requiem?

MOZART   I asked, 'Who is this Requiem for, who has died?' It said 'The work must be finished when you see me next!'

Then it turned and left the room!

SALIERI   Oh, this is morbid fancy, my friend!

MOZART   It had the force of real things! . . . To tell the truth – I
do not know whether it happened in my head or out of it . . .
No wonder Stanzi has gone. I frightened her away . . . And
now she'll miss the vaudeville.

SALIERI   You mean it's finished? So soon?

MOZART   Oh, yes – music is easy: it's marriage that's hard!

SALIERI   I long to see it!

MOZART   Would you come, truly? The theatre isn't grand. It's
just a popular music-hall. No one from Court will be there.

SALIERI   Do you think that matters to me? I would travel
anywhere for a work by you! . . . I am no substitute for your
little wife – but I know someone who could be!

He gets up. Mozart rises also.

MOZART   Who?

SALIERI   I'll tell you what – I'll bring Katherina! She'll cheer
you up!

MOZART   Katherina!

SALIERI   As I remember it, you quite enjoyed her company!

*Mozart laughs heartily. Cavalieri enters, now fatter and wearing an
elaborate plumed hat. She curtseys to Mozart and takes his arm.*

MOZART   (*bowing*) Signora!

SALIERI   (*to Audience*) And so to the opera we went – a strange
band of three!

The other two freeze.

The First Kapellmeister – sleek as a cat. His mistress – now
fat and feathered like a great songbird she'd become. And
Mozart, demented and drunk on the cheap wine which was
now his constant habit.

They unfreeze.

We went out into the suburbs – to a crowded music-hall – in

a tenement . . .

* * * *

The theatre by the Weiden

Two benches are brought in and placed down front. Sudden noise. A crowd of working-class Germans swarm in from the back: a chattering mass of humanity through which the three have to push their way to the front. The long table is pushed horizontally, and the rowdy audience piles on top of it, smoking pipes and chewing sausages.

Unobserved, Baron Van Swieten comes in also and stands at the back.

MOZART You must be indulgent now! It's my first piece of this kind!

The three sit on the front bench; Mozart sick and emaciated; Cavalieri blowsy and bedizened; Salieri as elegant as ever.

SALIERI We sat as he wished us to, among ordinary Germans! The smell of meat and sausage was almost annihilating!

Cavalieri presses a mouchoir to her sensitive nose.

(*To Mozart*) This is so exciting!

MOZART (*happily*) Do you think so?

SALIERI (*looking about him*) Oh yes! This is exactly the audience we should be writing for! Not the dreary Court . . . As always – *you* show the way!

The audience freezes.

(*To us*) As always, he did. My pungent neighbours *rolled* on their benches at the jokes –

They unfreeze – briefly to demonstrate this mirth.

And I alone in their midst heard – *The Magic Flute* !

They freeze again. The great hymn at the end of Act II is heard: 'Heil sei euch Geweihten'.

He had put the Masons into it right enough. Oh, yes – but

87

how? He had turned them into an Order of Eternal Priests. I heard voices calling out of ancient temples. I saw a vast sun rise on a timeless land, where animals danced and children floated: and by its rays all the poisons we feed each other drawn up and burnt away!

A great sun does indeed rise inside the Light Box, and standing in it the gigantic silhouette of a priestly figure extending its arms to the world in universal greeting.

And in this sun – behold – I saw his father. No more an accusing figure, but forgiving! The Highest Priest of the Order – his hand extended to the world in love! Wolfgang feared Leopold no longer: a final Legend has been made!... Oh the sound – the sound of that new-found peace in him – mocking my undiminishing pain! *There* was the Magic Flute – *there beside me*!

He points to Mozart. Applause from all. Mozart jumps up excitedly on to the bench and acknowledges the clapping with his arms flung out. He turns to us, a bottle in his hand – his eyes staring: all freeze again.

Mozart the flute, and God the relentless player. How long could the Creature stand it – so frail, so palpably mortal?... And what was this I was tasting suddenly? Could it be pity? ...*Never*!

VAN SWIETEN *(Calling out)* Mozart!

Van Swieten pushes his way to the front through the crowd of dispersing Citizens. He is outraged.

MOZART *(turning joyfully to greet him)* Baron! You here! How wonderful of you to come!

SALIERI *(to Audience)* I had of course suggested it.

VAN SWIETEN *(with cold fury)* What have you done?

MOZART Excellency?

VAN SWIETEN You have put our rituals into a vulgar show!

MOZART No, sir –

VAN SWIETEN They are plain for all to see! And to laugh at!

You have betrayed the Order.

MOZART *(in horror)* NO!

SALIERI Baron, a word with you –

VAN SWIETEN Don't speak for him, Salieri! *(To Mozart, with frozen contempt)* You were ever a cruel vulgarian we hoped to mend. Stupid, hopeless task! Now you are a betrayer as well. I shall never forgive you. And depend upon it – I shall ensure that no Freemason or Person of Distinction will do so in Vienna so long as I have life!

SALIERI Baron, please, I must speak!

VAN SWIETEN No, sir! Leave alone. *(To Mozart)* I did not look for this reward, Mozart. Never speak to me.

He goes out. The crowd disperses. The lights change. The benches are taken off. Salieri, watching Mozart narrowly, dismisses Katherina. Mozart stands as one dead.

SALIERI Wolfgang? . . .

Mozart shakes his head sharply – and walks away from him, upstage, desolate and stunned.

Wolfgang – all is not lost.

Mozart enters his apartment and freezes.

(To Audience) But of course it was! Now he was ruined. Broken and shunned by all men of influence. And for good measure, he did not even get his half receipts from the opera.

*   *   *   *

The Venticelli come in.

VENTICELLO 1 Schikaneder pays him nothing.

VENTICELLO 2 Schikaneder cheats him.

VENTICELLO 1 Gives him enough for liquor.

VENTICELLO 2 And keeps all the rest.

SALIERI I couldn't have managed it better myself.

Mozart takes up a blanket and muffles himself in it. Then he sits at his work-table, down front, staring out at the Audience, quite still, the blanket almost over his face.

And then silence. No word came from him at all. Why? . . . I waited each day. Nothing. Why? . . . *(to the Venticelli, brusquely)* *What does he do?*

Mozart writes.

VENTICELLO 1	He sits at his window.
VENTICELLO 2	All day and all night.
VENTICELLO 1	Writing –
VENTICELLO 2	Writing – like a man possessed.

Mozart springs to his feet, and freezes.

VENTICELLO 1	Springs up every moment!
VENTICELLO 2	Stares wildly at the street!
VENTICELLO 1	Expecting something –
VENTICELLO 2	Someone –

VENTICELLO 1 and VENTICELLO 2   *We can't imagine what!*
SALIERI   *(to Audience) I* could!

He also springs up excitedly, dismissing the Venticelli. Mozart and Salieri now both stand staring out front.

Who did he look for? A Figure in grey, masked and sorrowing, come to take him away. I knew what he was doing, alone in that slum! He was writing his Requiem Mass – *for himself!* *(Pause)* . . . And now I confess the wickedest thing I did to him.

His Valet brings him the clothes which he describes, and he puts them on, turning his back to us to don the hat – to which is attached a mask.

My friends – there is no blasphemy a man will not commit, compelled to such a war as mine! . . . I got me a cloak of grey . . . Yes. I got me a hat of grey. Yes. And a mask of grey – Yes!

He turns round: he is masked.

And appeared myself to the demented Creature as – the *Messenger of God!* ... I confess that in November 1791, I – Antonio Salieri, then as now First Royal Kapellmeister to the Empire – walked empty Vienna in the freezing moonlight for seven nights on end! That precisely as the clocks of the city struck one I would halt beneath Mozart's window – and become his more terrible clock.

The clock strikes one. Salieri, without moving from the left side of the stage, raises his arms: his fingers show seven days. Mozart rises – fascinated and appalled – and stands equally rigidly on the right side, looking out in horror.

Every night I showed him one day less – then stalked away. Every night the face he showed me at the glass was more crazed. Finally – with no days left to him – *horror*! I arrived as usual. Halted. And instead of fingers, reached up beseechingly as the Figure of his dreams! 'Come! – Come! – Come! ...'

He beckons to Mozart, insidiously.

He stood swaying, as if he would faint off into death. But suddenly – incredibly – he realized all his little strength, and in a clear voice called down to me the words out of his opera *Don Giovanni*, inviting the statue to dinner.

MOZART *(pushing open the 'window')* O statua gentilissima – venite a cena!

He beckons in his turn.

SALIERI For a long moment one terrified man looked at another. Then – unbelievably – I found myself nodding, just as in the opera. Starting to move across the street!

The rising and falling scale passage from the Overture to Don Giovanni *sounds darkly, looped in sinister repetition. To this hollow music Salieri marches slowly upstage.*

Pushing down the latch of his door – tramping up the stairs with stone feet. There was no stopping it. *I was in his dream!*

91

Mozart stands terrified by his table. Salieri throws open the door. An instant light change.

Salieri stands still, staring impassively downstage. Mozart addresses him urgently, and in awe.

MOZART It's not finished!... Not nearly!... Forgive me. Time was I could write a Mass in a week!... Give me one month more and it'll be done: I swear it!... He'll grant me that, surely? You can't want it unfinished!... Look – Look, see what I've done.

He snatches up the pages from the table and brings them eagerly to the Figure.

Here's the Kyrie – that's finished! Take that to Him – He'll see it's not unworthy!... Kyrie the first theme, Eleison the second. Both together make a double fugue.

Unwillingly Salieri moves across the room – takes the pages, and sits behind the table in Mozart's chair, staring out front.

Grant me time, I beg you! If you do, I swear I'll write a real piece of music. I know I've boasted I've written hundreds, but it's not true. I've written nothing finally good!

Salieri looks at the pages. Immediately we hear the sombre opening of the Requiem Mass. Over this Mozart speaks.

Oh, it began so well, my life. Once the world was so full, so happy!... All the journeys – all the carriages – all the rooms of smiles! Everyone smiled at me once – the King at Schönbrunn; the Princess at Versailles – they lit my way with candles to the clavier! – my father bowing, bowing, bowing with such joy!... 'Chevalier Mozart, my miraculous son!' ... Why has it all gone?... Why?... Was I so bad? So wicked... (*Desperately*) Answer for Him and tell me!

Deliberately Salieri tears the paper into halves. The music stops instantly. Silence.

(*fearfully*) Why? . . . Is it not good?

SALIERI   (*stiffly*) It is good. Yes. It is good.

He tears off a corner of the music paper, elevates it in the manner of the Communion Service, places it on his tongue and eats it.

(*in pain*) I eat what God gives me. Dose after dose. For all of life. His poison. We are both poisoned, Amadeus. I with you: you with me.

In horror Mozart moves slowly behind him, placing his hand over Salier's mouth — then, still from behind, slowly removes the mask and hat. Salieri stares at us.

Eccomi. Antonio Salieri. Ten years of my hate have poisoned you to death.

Mozart falls to his knees, by the table.

MOZART   Oh God!

SALIERI   (*contemptuously*) God?! . . . God will not help you! God *does* not help!

MOZART   Oh God! . . . Oh God! . . . Oh God!

SALIERI   God does not love you, Amadeus! God does not love! He can only *use*! . . . He cares nothing for who He uses: nothing for who He denies! . . . You are no use to Him any more — you're too weak — too sick! He has finished with you! All you can do now is *die*! He'll find another instrument! He won't even remember you!

MOZART   *Ah!*

With a groan Mozart crawls quickly through the trestle of the table, like an animal finding a burrow — or a child a safe place of concealment. Salieri kneels by the table, calling in at his victim in desperation.

SALIERI   . . . Die, Amadeus! Die, I beg you, die! . . . Leave me alone, *ti imploro!* Leave me alone at last! Leave me alone!

He beats on the table in his despair.

Alone! Alone! Alone! Alone! Alone!

MOZART (*crying out at the top of his lungs*) PAPAAAAA!

He freezes – his mouth open in the act of screaming – his head staring out from under the table.

Salieri rises in horror. Silence. Then very slowly, Mozart crawls out from under the table. He sits. He sees Salieri. He smiles at him.

(*in a childish voice*) Papa!

Silence.

Papa . . . Papa . . .

He extends his arms upwards, imploringly to Salieri. He speaks now as a very young boy.

Take me, Papa. Take me. Put down your arms and I'll hop into them. Just as we used to do it! . . . Hop-hop-hop-UP!

He jumps up on to the table, and embraces Salieri who stands in horror.

Hold me close to you, Papa. Let's sing our little Kissing Song together. Do you remember? . . .

He sings in an infantine voice.

Oragna figata fa! Marina gamina fa!

Gently Salieri disengages himself.

SALIERI Reduce the man: reduce the God. Behold my vow fulfilled. The profoundest voice in the world reduced to a nursery tune.

He leaves the room, slowly, as Mozart resumes his singing.

MOZART Oragna figata fa! Marina gamina fa!

As Salieri withdraws, Constanze appears from the back of the stage, her bonnet in her hand. She has returned from Baden. She comes downstage towards her husband, and finds him there on the table, singing in an obviously childish treble.

Oragna figata fa! Marina gamina fa. Fa! Fa!

He kisses the air, several times. Finally he becomes aware of his wife standing beside him.

    (*uncertainly*) Stanzi?

CONSTANZE Wolfi? . . .

MOZART (*in relief*) Stanzi!

CONSTANZE (*with great tenderness*) Wolfi – my love! Little husband of my heart!

He virtually falls off the table into her arms.

MOZART Oh!

He clings to her in overwhelming pleasure. She helps him gently to move behind it, facing out front.

CONSTANZE Oh, my dear one – come with me . . . Come on . . . Come on now. There . . . There . . .

Mozart sits weakly.

MOZART (*like a child still, and most earnestly*) Salieri . . . Salieri has killed me.

CONSTANZE Yes, my dear.

Practically she busies herself clearing the table of its candle, its bottle and its inkwell.

MOZART He has. He told me so.

CONSTANZE Yes, yes: I'm sure.

She finds two pillows and places them at the left-hand head of the table.

MOZART (*petulantly*) He did . . . He did!

CONSTANZE Hush now, lovey.

She helps her dying husband on to the table, now his bed. He lies down, and she covers him with her shawl.

    I'm back to take care of you. I'm sorry I went away. I'm here now, for always!

MOZART Salieri . . . Salieri . . . Salieri . . . Salieri!

He starts to weep.

CONSTANZE   Oh lovey, be silent now. No one has hurt you. You'll get better soon, I promise. Can you hear me? Try to, Wolferl . . . Wolfi-polfi, please! . . .

Faintly the Lacrimosa of the Requiem Mass begins to sound. Mozart rises to hear it – leaning against his wife's shoulders. His hand begins feebly to beat out drum measures from the music. During the whole of the following it is evident that he is composing the Mass in his head, and does not hear his wife at all.

If I've been a bore – if I've nagged a bit about money, it didn't mean anything. It's only because I'm spoilt. You spoilt me, lovey. You've got to get well, Wolfi – because we need you. Karl and Baby Franz as well. There's only the three of us, lovey: we don't cost much. Just don't leave us – we wouldn't know what to do without you. And you wouldn't know much either, up in Heaven, without us. You soppy thing. You can't even cut up your own meat without help! . . . I'm not clever, lovey. It can't have been easy living with a goose. But I've looked after you, you must admit that. And I've given you fun too – quite a lot really! . . . Are you listening?

The drum strokes get slower, and stop.

Know one thing. It was the best day of my life when you married me. And as long as I live I'll be the most honoured woman in the world . . . Can you hear me?

She becomes aware that Mozart is dead. She opens her mouth in a silent scream, raising her arm in a rigid gesture of grief.
    The great chord of the 'Amen' does not resolve itself, but lingers on in intense reverberation.

*   *   *   *

Citizens of Vienna come in, dressed in black, from the right. Constanze kneels and freezes in grief, as Servants come in and stand at each of the

*four corners of the table on which the dead body lies. Van Swieten also
comes in.*

SALIERI *(hard)* The Death Certificate said kidney failure,
hastened by exposure to cold. Generous Lord Fugue paid
for a pauper's funeral. Twenty other corpses. An unmarked
limepit.

Van Swieten approaches Constanze.

VAN SWIETEN What little I can spare, you shall have for the
children. There's no need to waste it on vain show.

*The Servants lift the table and bear it, with its burden, upstage, centre,
to the Light Box. The Citizens follow it.*

SALIERI What did I feel? Relief, of course: I confess it. And
pity too, for the man I helped to destroy. I felt the pity God
can never feel. I weakened God's flute to thinness. God blew
– as He must – without cease. The flute split in the mouth of
His insatiable *need!*

*The Citizens kneel. In dead silence the Servants throw Mozart's body
off the table into the space at the back of the stage.*
*All depart save Salieri and Constanze. She unfreezes and starts
assiduously collecting the manuscripts scattered over the floor.*
*Salieri now speaks with an increasingly ageing voice: a voice poisoned
more and more by his own bitterness.*

As for Constanze, in the fullness of time she married again –
a Danish diplomat as dull as a clock – and retired to Salzburg,
birthplace of the Great Composer, to become the final
authority in all matters Mozartian!

*Constanze rises, wrapping her shawl about her, and clasping manuscripts
to her bosom.*

CONSTANZE *(reverentially)* A sweeter-tongued man never lived!
In ten years of blissful marriage I never heard him utter a
single coarse or conceited word. The purity of his life is reflected

97

absolutely in the purity of his music!... (*More briskly*) In selling his manuscripts I charge by the ink. So many notes, so many schillings. That seems to me the simplest way.

She leaves the stage, a pillar of rectitude.

SALIERI One amazing fact emerged. Mozart did not *imagine* that masked Figure in grey who said, 'Take up your pen and write a Requiem'. It was *real*!... A certain bizarre nobleman called Count Walsegg had a longing to be thought a composer. He actually sent his Steward in disguise to Mozart to commission the piece – secretly, so that he could pass it off as his own work. And this he even did! After Mozart's death it was actually performed as Count Walsegg's Requiem... And I conducted it.

He smiles at the Audience.

Naturally I did. In those days I presided over all great musical occasions in Vienna.

He divests himself of his cloak.

I even conducted the salvoes of cannon in Beethoven's dreadful *Battle Symphony*. An experience which made me almost as deaf as he was!

The Citizens turn round and bow to him, kissing their hands extravagantly.

And so I stayed on in the City of Musicians, reverenced by all! *On* and *on* and *on*!... *For thirty-two years!*... And slowly I understood the nature of God's punishment. (*Directly, to the Audience*) What had I asked for in that Church as a boy? Was it not Fame? Well now I had it! I was to become quite simply the most famous musician in Europe!... I was to be bricked up in Fame! Buried in Fame!... Embalmed in Fame – but for work I knew to be absolutely worthless!... This was my sentence! I must endure thirty years of being called 'distinguished' – by people incapable of distinguishing!

The Citizens have fallen on their knees to him during the preceding, and are all clapping their hands at him silently in an adoring mime, relentlessly extending their arms upwards and upwards until they seem almost to obliterate him.

I must smell as I wrote it the deadness of my music, whilst their eyes brimmed with tears and their throats brayed with cheering! . . . And finally – when my nose had been rubbed in Fame to vomiting – receptions, awards, civic medals and chains: suddenly His Masterstroke! – *Silence!*

The Citizens freeze.

It would all be taken away from me – every scrap.

The Citizens rise, turn away from him, and walk indifferently offstage.

Mozart's music would sound everywhere – and mine in no place on earth. I must survive to see myself become *extinct!* . . . When they trundled me out in a carriage to get my last honour a man on the kerb said 'Isn't that one of the Generals from Waterloo?' *(Calling up savagely.) Nemico dei Nemici! Dio implacabile!*

The curtains close. The wheelchair is brought on by a Servant. Another hands Salieri his old dressing gown and cap, as he divests himself of his wig and becomes once more the old man.

The lights change. Six o'clock strikes. We are back in:

*   *   *   *

Salieri's apartment

The Servants leave.

SALIERI Dawn has come. I must release you. One moment's violence and it is over. You see, I cannot accept this. To be sucked into oblivion – not even my name remembered. Oh no. I did not live on earth to be His joke for eternity. I have one trick left me – see how He deals with this! *(Confidentially, to Audience)* All this week I have been shouting out about murder. You heard me yourselves – do you remember?

'Mozart – *pietà!* Pardon your Assassin! Mozart!'

Whispers of 'Salieri' begin: at first faintly, as at the start of the play. During the following they grow in volume, in strict and operatic counter-point to Salieri's speeches.

WHISPERERS *(faintly)* Salieri!

SALIERI *(triumphantly)* I did this deliberately!... My servants carried the news into the streets!

WHISPERERS *(louder)* Salieri!

SALIERI The streets repeated it to one another!

WHISPERERS *(louder)* Salieri!... Salieri!

SALIERI Now my name is on every tongue! Vienna, City of Scandals, has a scandal worthy of it at last!

WHISPERERS SALIERI! ... ASSASSIN! ... ASSASSIN! ... SALIERI!

SALIERI *(falsetto: enjoying it)* 'Can it be true?... Is it possible? Did he do it after all?' ...

WHISPERERS *(fortissimo)* SALIERI!!!

SALIERI Well, my friends, now they all will know for sure! They will learn of my dreadful death – and they will believe the lie forever! After today, whenever men speak Mozart's name with love, they will speak mine with loathing! As his name grows in the world so will mine – if not in fame, then in infamy. *I'm going to be immortal after all!* – And He is powerless to prevent it!... *(He laughs harshly.)* So, Signore – see now if Man is mocked!

He produces a razor from his pocket. Then he rises, opens it, and addresses the Audience most simply, gently, and directly.

Amici cari. I was born a pair of ears, and nothing else. It is only through hearing music that I know God exists. Only through writing music that I could worship.... All around me men hunger for General Rights. I hungered only for particular notes. They seek Liberty for Mankind. I sought only slavery for myself. To be owned – ordered – exhausted by an Absolute. This was denied me – and with it all meaning.

Now I go to become a ghost myself. I will stand in the shadows when you come here to this earth in your turn. And when you feel the dreadful bite of your failures – and hear the taunting of unachievable, uncaring God – I will whisper my name to you: 'Antonio Salieri: Patron Saint of Mediocrities!' And in the depth of your downcastness you can pray to me. And I will forgive you. *Vi saluto.*

He cuts his throat and falls backwards into the wheelchair.

The Cook – who has just entered carrying a plate of buns for breakfast, screams in horror. The Valet rushes in at the same time from the other side. Together they pull the wheelchair, with its slumped body, backwards upstage, and anchor it in the centre.

The Venticelli appear again, in the costume of 1823.

VENTICELLO 1 Beethoven's Conversation Book, November 1823. Visitors write the news for the deaf man.

He hands a book to Venticello 2.

VENTICELLO 2 (*reading*) 'Salieri has cut his throat – but is still alive!'

Salieri stirs and comes to life, looking about him bewilderedly. The Valet and the Cook depart. He stares out front like an astounded gargoyle.

VENTICELLO 1 Beethoven's Conversation Book, 1824. Visitors write the news for the deaf man.

He hands another book to Venticello 2.

VENTICELLO 2 (*reading*) 'Salieri is quite deranged. He keeps claiming that he is guilty of Mozart's death, and made away with him by poison.'

The light narrows into a bright cone, beating on Salieri.

VENTICELLO 1 The *German Musical Times*, May 25th 1825.

He hands a newspaper to Venticello 2.

VENTICELLO 2 (*reading*) 'Our worthy Salieri just cannot die. In the frenzy of his imagination he is even said to accuse himself of complicity in Mozart's early death. A rambling of the mind believed in truth by no one but the deluded old man himself.'

The music stops.

Salieri lowers his head, conceding defeat.

VENTICELLO 1   I don't believe it.
VENTICELLO 2   I don't believe it.
VENTICELLO 1   I don't believe it.
VENTICELLO 2   I don't believe it.
VENTICELLO 1 and VENTICELLO 2   *No one believes it in the world!*

They go off. The light dims a little. Salieri stirs – raises his head – and looks out far into the darkness of the theatre.

SALIERI   Mediocrities everywhere – now and to come – I absolve you all. Amen!

He extends his arms upwards and outwards to embrace the assembled Audience in a wide gesture of Benediction – finally folding his arms high across his own breast.

The light fades completely. The last four chords of the Masonic Funeral Music of Amadeus Mozart sound throughout the theatre.

END OF PLAY

SALIERI'S MARCH as played by both Salieri and Mozart, Mozart playing it faster, lighter, and less decoratively.

MOZART'S TRANSFORMATION PROCESS:

'It doesn't really work, that fourth – does it?'

'Let's try the third above...'   'Ah yes!...'

'NON PIÚ ANDRAI' arranged for piano by Kevin Leeman
At first tentatively

Notes

The notes in this edition are intended to serve the needs of overseas students as well as those of British-born users.
*Notes on stage directions are indicated by quotation marks.

The set

xxix *'Rococo'**: style of architecture and design characterized by a proliferation of ornamental detail (such as shells, scrolls, unsymmetrical curves and so on) which was superimposed on the structure rather than being made an integral part of it: flourished notably in France during the reign of Louis XV (1715–74).

'salon': drawing room, reception room.

'proscenium': wide archway framing (in this case) the rear of the stage.

'Palace of Schönbrunn': large palace built for the imperial Austrian family by the great architect Fischer von Erlach in the early years of the eighteenth century.

'Joseph II': (1741–90) became joint ruler of Austria with his mother, the Empress Maria Theresa, after the death of his father in 1765. See also note to *Maria Theresa*, page 21.

xxx *'fortepiano'*: the eighteenth-century name given to an early type of piano: a keyboard instrument whose stretched and tuned wires are struck by hammers attached to the keys.

Act One

1 *'Vienna'*: in 1823 capital of the Austrian Empire and centre of the musical world.

Salieri: Antonio (1750–1825) – Italian composer who settled in Vienna and lived there for fifty years. Pupil of Gluck, teacher of Beethoven and Schubert.

'*the scene ... Overture*': see *Introduction* pages xxi–xxii for a discussion of the structure of this scene. An overture is a piece of instrumental music intended as the introduction to an opera or oratorio. In the late eighteenth century, the Bavarian composer Gluck (who is mentioned several times in the course of *Amadeus*) set a fashion, followed by Mozart himself, of using the overtures to his operas to prepare the audience for the dramatic action that was to follow. Shaffer's opening scene is nothing if not an overture in this precise sense.

2 *the Opera:* the present opera house in Vienna was opened in 1869, prior to which date all important operatic productions took place in the Burgtheater, which now serves as the state theatre for spoken drama.

the Prater: it was Jospeh II – the emperor in *Amadeus* – who gave this immense area of grass and woodland that had once been a hunting reserve for the aristocracy to the people of Vienna. Here they might drive or stroll or dance and sing at one of the many cafés that soon became established.

Metternich: Prince Clemens Lothar Wenzel (1773–1859) – distinguished Austrian statesman and diplomat.

Beethoven: Ludwig van (1770–1827) – German composer who was resident for most of his life in Vienna. As well as Salieri, he numbered among his teachers Haydn and Mozart. Soon after the age of 30 he began to lose his hearing and by the end of his life was completely deaf (see closing scene of the play, page 101): this disability did not, however, prevent his attaining the greatest heights as a composer.

3 *Kapellmeister:* originally the term *kapelle* was used to describe the entire musical staff (including clergy, singers, instrumentalists) employed in a royal chapel. Later, it came to mean any organized group of musicians employed at court. The *kapellmeister* was the director or conductor of a *kapelle*.

recluse: someone who shuts himself away from society.

4 *Thirty-two ... dying:* Mozart died on 5 December 1791, a fact

which establishes the year of the present scene as 1823.

Syphilis: it is part of the enduring mystery surrounding Mozart's life that no one really knows the cause of his death. Some certainly say it was venereal disease, others mental exhaustion, and others typhus or kidney failure or uraemia. Yet others hold fast to the poisoning theory ...

5 *Vi Saluto! ... a vostro servizio!: (Italian)* I greet you, ghosts of the future! Antonio Salieri – at your service!

Salieri looks more than a century and a half into the future, addressing the numberless audiences who, out of the darkness of the theatres in which they are seated, will watch the enactment of his story.

smallest hours: earliest hours of the morning.

Confessors: priests who listen while parishioners recount in strict privacy the sins they have committed, and then grant them forgiveness.

6 *capricious:* unpredictable, changeable.

Via ... Grazie!: (Italian) Go. Go, go, go! Thank you!

Invocation: musical set-piece, common in the operas of the late eighteenth century, by means of which gods or spirits or the ghosts of the dead were supposed to be summoned up.

'figurations ... Recitativo Secco': recitative is a type of musical composition for the solo voice – featuring in opera and oratorio – in which the natural rhythms and inflexions of the spoken word take precedence over considerations of melody. *Recitativo Secco* (literally, 'dry recitative') is especially quick moving and has a background of simple chords suggested by a figured bass as accompaniment.

Incarnation: appearance in the flesh, in living form.

7 *Posterity:* the generations to be born in the future.

Chevalier Gluck: Christoph Willibald von Gluck (1714–87) – Bavarian composer, noted for his innovations in the field of opera, who lived much of his working life in Vienna. He is mentioned several times in the course of the play. *Chevalier* was a courtesy title used by gentlemen on whom the distinction of knighthood had been conferred – equivalent to the modern 'Sir –'.

Rossini: Gioacchino Antonio (1792–1868) – Italian opera composer noted particularly for his melodic gift and his sense of humour. Salieri's comment on 'the antics of hairdressers' is a direct reference to Rossini's highly successful comic opera *Il Barbiere di Siviglia* ('The Barber of Seville') which received its first performance in 1816.

Scusate: (*Italian*) Excuse me.

Gluttony: – the love of excessive eating – is one of the seven deadly sins that good Christians are supposed to shun. Salieri is beginning his confession to the audience, the ghosts of the future, on a rather trivial note.

Infantine: childish.

Milanese: from Milan, important city in Northern Italy.

Sienna: Italian city famed for its cakes and confectionery.

macaroons: sweet biscuits made of almonds.

pistachio: type of nut – with a flavour similar to that of the almond – common in the Mediterranean area.

Italian subjects ... Austrian Empire: at different times in its history, the Austrian Empire incorporated large areas of territory beyond the boundaries of modern Austria. Hungary, in particular, was part of this empire, as were parts of Czechoslovakia and Northern Italy.

Lombardy: province in the extreme north of Italy.

Hapsburg: though the Hapsburg family originated in Switzerland, its members ruled the Austrian Empire without interruption from the late thirteenth century until 1918.

8 *firmament:* heaven.

aria: piece of music for a solo singer with accompaniment; like the recitative (see note on *Recitativo Secco*), another operatic stereotype.

anthem: choral music composed for church use.

The Christs of Lombardy ... candle-smoked God: in remembering the wall-paintings in the Lombardy churches of his youth, Salieri points the contrast between representations of the harsh, vengeful Old Testament God, and those of the New

Testament Christ, God of love and forgiveness, His sleeve embroidered with the emblem of the Lamb, the symbol of meekness.

mulberry: dark purple – the colour of the mulberry fruit.

Signore: (*Italian*) Lord.

Bene: (*Italian*) Good.

9 *prodigy:* child of amazing talent, young genius.

virtuoso: musician of the highest technical skill.

'soutane': cassock, ankle-length robe worn by a priest.

'Bonno': Giuseppe (1710–88) – minor Italian composer who settled, like so many other musicians, in Vienna in order to further his career.

10 *The age ... Enlightenment:* period – from about 1745 to 1790 – marked by a spirit of questioning and striving after new ideas not only in the arts, but also in the realms of philosophy and science.

that clear time ... in half: the period before the French Revolution which erupted in 1789. The guillotine was adopted as a means of executing the enemies of the revolution in 1791.

Katherina Cavalieri: celebrated singer of the period much associated with the music of both Salieri and Mozart.

to depress her diaphragm: a singing teacher might well put pressure with his fingertips on his pupil's diaphragm (or midriff – the area of the body separating the chest from the abdomen) as a way of teaching proper breath control and voice production.

11 *sacramentalized their mediocrity:* gave a special dignity or grace to the ordinariness of their lives.

strings divisi: (music played by) a group of stringed instruments, including violins, violas and 'cellos.

chittarini: plural of *chitarrone* (or archlute), a large stringed instrument with a long neck, played – like a guitar – by plucking.

serenades: light music, for performance of an evening or at night, usually out of doors. Mozart composed many serenades.

rutting: love-making.

Trumpets sounded . . . they left it!: fanfares of trumpets were a common means of heralding a royal birth, while the more sombre sounds of trombones were frequently associated with funerals.

'icons': stylized religious portraits, found especially in Orthodox churches.

12 *Salzburg:* important Austrian city about 180 miles (290 kilometres) west of Vienna. In Mozart's day, it was ruled by a prince archbishop who exercised considerable secular as well as spiritual authority. Mozart was born in Salzburg in 1756 and it remained the home to which he habitually returned from his extensive travels, up to the time of his settling in Vienna in 1781. Like his father, he was employed in the archbishop's *kapelle* for some years.

symphony: large-scale orchestral work, usually – at this period – in four contrasting movements.

concerto: (usually) three-movement work in which a solo instrument (such as a piano or violin) is accompanied by the orchestra. Mozart was the greatest of the concerto composers in its classical period.

opera: musical drama, one in which the majority – if not all – of the words are set to music.

Mitridate, King of Pontus: received its first performance in Milan on 26 December 1770, when Mozart was indeed still only fourteen.

'Schönbrunn': see note to page xxix on *'Palace of Schönbrunn'*.

Chamberlain: high-ranking official responsible for the organization and running of the imperial household.

13 *Director of the Opera:* intendant, official in charge of the general administration of the opera house and performances given there.

Prefect of the Imperial Library: court official responsible for the maintenance of the Library.

Freemason: member of the Order of Freemasons, a secret

organization or brotherhood divided into local groups or 'lodges', whose members are pledged to help each other in times of trouble.

Fugue: type of musical composition in which a theme or 'subject' is stated by one voice and then immediately taken up by a second, during which the first voice goes on to provide an accompaniment to the theme. Third, fourth, fifth (and further) voices may also be involved, according to the complexity of the music. Fugues were highly popular among composers of the generations preceding Salieri and Mozart and were – to some extent – considered to be rather old-fashioned: hence Salieri's remark about Baron van Swieten.

Idomeneo: Mozart's opera had been given its first performance on 29 January 1781 in Munich.

Leopold Mozart: (1719–87) – *kapellmeister* (see note to page 3) to the Archbishop of Salzburg, Hieronymus Colloredo (see also note to page 12 on *Salzburg*).

non è vero, Compositore?: (*Italian*) isn't that so, Court Composer?

Note that at this stage of the action, Salieri is not yet *kapellmeister*, but occupies the inferior position of Court Composer. See page 10 for an expression of his anxiety to obtain Bonno's post.

Divengono sempre sterili con gli anni: (*Italian*) They always grow barren as years go by.

Precisamente: (*Italian*) Exactly.

Niente, Signor Pomposo: (*Italian*) Nothing, Mr Pompous. There is plainly little real friendship between Strack and Rosenberg.

14 *Lodge:* see note to page 13 on *Freemason*.

Peter Platz: square near the centre of Vienna.

Madame Weber: Cäcilia Weber was, by the time in question, a widow, rather too fond of drink, who manipulated her 'tribe of daughters' towards advantageous marriages with a firm hand.

Aloysia: Mozart had met Aloysia Weber – the eldest of four sisters – in the German city of Mannheim towards the end of 1777 and had fallen head-over-heels in love with her. He had been desolated at having to part from her in March of the following year. Their paths crossed again in November 1778, but by now Aloysia had grown cold towards Mozart. By the time of their meeting in Vienna in 1781, she had married a painter and actor named Josef Lange.

15 *Baroness Waldstädten:* Cäcilia Weber had so contrived to compromise her second daughter, Constanze, with Mozart, and to arrange matters in such a way that marriage was the only course possible for the two young people, that even Constanze became sickened by her manipulation. Consequently, she took up residence in the house of the Baroness Waldstädten, who was one of Mozart's patrons.

Restiamo in contatto: (*Italian*) Let us keep in touch.

Certamente, Signore: (*Italian*) Certainly, sir.

Sorbetti: water-ices.

caramelli: egg custards flavoured with a sauce made of burnt sugar.

16 *'knee-breeches':* trousers which reached and were fastened just below the knee.

I'm going to pounce-bounce . . . : see *Introduction*, pages xiv–xv, for a discussion of Mozart's language, both in the play and in real life.

17 *Stanzerl . . . Wolferl:* homely Austrian contractions of 'Constanze' and 'Wolfgang' respectively: the language of those who have little time for or interest in the elevated ways of courtiers.

18 *'major-domo':* official entrusted with the organization of a large household.

'imperviously': as if he had not noticed what was going on in the room.

Serenade: see note to page 11 on *serenades*.

19 *Adagio:* piece of music intended to be played at a slow speed.

bassoons . . . basset horns . . . oboe . . . clarinets: different types of wind instruments.

squeezebox: concertina.

'rent': with gaps, as it were, torn through the clouds.

20 *salon:* see note to page xxix.

Motets: vocal or, more usually, choral music to Latin texts intended for church use.

Anthems: see note to page 8 on *anthem.*

sonata: composition of three or more movements, usually intended to be played on one instrument.

Munich: capital of Bavaria, now part of West Germany. Mozart had paid his first visit there – with his father and family – in 1762, when he was six. He returned to the city on a number of occasions later in his career.

Mannheim: German city, situated on the River Rhine. See also note to page 14 on *Aloysia.*

Parisian Symphony: Mozart had visited the French capital several times during his life, notably in 1778 after leaving Mannheim (see note to page 14 on *Aloysia*). It was as a result of this visit that he composed his so-called 'Paris' Symphony (No 31 in D).

Divertimento: literally an 'amusement' piece; like the serenade (see note to page 11) and the *Cassazione*, it was light music – a suite or series of contrasting movements, sometimes intended for outdoor performance.

Cassazione: see note to *Divertimento* above.

21 *Litany:* choral work for church use, of a mainly penitential nature.

swanky: show-off.

Fêtes: not the sort that are held of an English summer afternoon on the vicarage lawn, but a lavish eighteenth-century festivity, usually associated with a saint's day and marked with music, dancing, feasting and firework displays.

Je suis follement impatient!: (*French*) I'm madly impatient!

Maria Theresa: (1717–80) – Queen of Hungary and Bohemia, and Empress of Austria in her own right. After the death of her husband in 1765 she continued to rule with the aid of the son who eventually succeeded her (as the Emperor

113

Joseph II).

Marie Antoinette: (1755–93) – daughter of Maria Theresa (see note above) and wife of Louis XVI of France. Died on the guillotine (see note to page 10 on *that clear time . . . in half*) after being captured and imprisoned by the revolutionaries.

22 *Mon Dieu:* (*French*) My God (used as a mild oath).

I wish . . . virtuoso: Mozart did in fact take part in a number of such competitions during his lifetime – on 24 December 1781 he and the composer Clementi pitted their skills as pianists against one another in the presence of Joseph II.

Court Composer: see note to page 13 on *non è vero, Compositore?*

allons!: (*French*) proceed (to play), let's go!

'surcoat': outer coat, usually without sleeves, worn over ordinary dress.

'dress-sword': gentlemen were expected, in the late eighteenth century, to wear swords as part of formal attire.

'banal': commonplace, dull.

Comme d'habitude!: (*French*) As ever!

23 *Non . . . plaît:* (*French*) No, no, please!

levez-vous!: (*French*) get up!

My sister remembers . . . '. . . yes or no?': the story recounted here by Joseph is a well-known part of Mozart folklore. Marie Antoinette would have been about seven at the time, 1762.

purler: blow resulting from a heavy fall.

Finalmente . . . straordinario: (*Italian*) At last! What a delight! What an amazing pleasure!

24 *Grazie Signore! . . . brillante e famosissimo!:* (*Italian*) Thank you, Sir! A thousand thousand welcomes! I am overwhelmed! It is an extraordinary honour to meet you! Such a brilliant and famous composer!

libretto: text set to music in an opera.

Stephanie: Gottlieb – actor at the National Theatre in Vienna, as well as writer. He later also collaborated with Mozart over his entertainment *Der Schauspieldirektor* ('The Impressario') in 1786.

seraglio: harem, women's quarters in a moslem house.

25 *pasha:* in Turkey (until 1934) title given to a provincial governor.

cattivo: (*Italian*) nasty, bad: 'You are making mischief, Court Composer.'

male sopranos: though today we may tend to associate the high soprano voice with young boys and women, in Mozart's day and earlier it was not uncommon for grown men who had been castrated at puberty to be trained to sing in this register.

Au revoir . . . à la court: (*French*) Goodbye for now, Mr Mozart. Welcome to the Court.

Majesté! – je suis comblé . . . de mes dûs!: (*French*) Your Majesty, I'm overwhelmed at the honour of being made welcome in the household of the Father of all musicians. To serve a monarch as full of discernment as Your Majesty is an honour which surpasses my highest deserving.

26 *'aside':* speech intended to be heard by the audience but not by any of the other characters on the stage.

27 *'reprise':* repeat.

Grazie ancora: (*Italian*) Thank you again.

'Fourth' . . . 'Third': in music the difference in pitch between any two notes is called an *interval*. The size of any interval is expressed in numerical terms: thus, from C to F is a *fourth*, because if we start playing at C on a piano keyboard and then proceed up the scale to F we will have covered four notes in all. Likewise, a *third* is an interval of three notes (say, C to E).

'arpeggio': chord which has been spread out so that its constituent notes are heard in succession rather than all at once.

'The Marriage of Figaro': Mozart's opera *Le Nozze di Figaro* was first performed in Vienna in 1786 (see pages 68–70). 'Non più andrai' is an aria in the first act in which Figaro tells the page Cherubino, who is about to be sent off to join the army, that he must get used to the idea of putting the pleasures and advantages of his present way of life behind him. The march-like character of the piece is very much in

keeping with the context in which it is heard. The introduction of the tune at this particular point in the play serves as an ironic warning to Salieri that *his* way of life is about to be rudely changed (see also *Introduction*, page xix). *'treble'*: the topmost line in the music.

28 *Variation*: piece of music entailing the transformation of a given theme by means of such devices as florid elaboration, change of speed or key, and so on.

Danaius: in Greek mythology, Danaius pretends to end a feud by giving his fifty daughters in marriage to the fifty sons of his old enemy. Secretly, however, he orders them to murder their husbands on their wedding-night and all but one do so. This is the crime for which he is punished.

29 *The Abduction from the Seraglio*: Mozart's opera *Die Entführung aus dem Serail* was first performed on 16 July 1782.

'Marten aller Arten': aria from Act 2 of *Die Entführung* in which the heroine Constanze declares that nothing – not even torture or the threat of death – will prevail upon her to yield to the Pasha.

scale: succession of notes played or sung in ascending or descending order of pitch; often used as a technical exercise.

he'd had her: (*slang*) he had had sexual intercourse with her.

'Finale': closing movement or section of a piece of music.

'flounces': strips sewn to the skirt of a dress by their upper edge and allowed to hang loosely.

30 *Enchanté, Fraulein*: I'm delighted to meet you, young lady. Joseph's combination of French and German words reminds us of the surface cosmopolitanism of his court.

Too many notes ... as are required: this exchange between Joseph and Mozart is based on an actual conversation they are supposed to have had after a performance of *Die Entführung*.

31 *The Pope ... wetting my bed*: it was in 1770, when Mozart was fourteen, that Pope Clement XIV had bestowed on him the Order of the Golden Spur, entitling him henceforward to call himself Chevalier Mozart – though he did so only very

infrequently.

cara: (*Italian*) dear.

32 *un tesoro raro!:* (*Italian*) a rare treasure!

33 *Mozart and Weber – married!:* Mozart's marriage to Constanze Weber took place at St Stephen's, in Vienna, on 4 August 1782.

Wipplingerstrasse: street in what was, in Mozart's time, a moderately fashionable district of Vienna.

wops: (*slang*) disrespectful term for 'foreigners', especially Italians.

34 *Tonic and dominant:* the simplest, most basic musical idea. The *tonic* is the key-note, that on which the key of a piece of music is based; the *dominant* is that note which comes at the interval of a fifth above the tonic (thus, where C is the tonic, G is the dominant). See also note to page 27 on *'Fourth'* ... *'Third'*.

modulation: change of key in the course of a passage of music.

chromatic passage: one in which the melody progresses by semi-tones (using sharps and flats) while remaining in the original key.

'Falsetto': in a high-pitched voice, like a woman's.

Morboso! ... *Nervoso!* ... *Ohimè!:* (*Italian*) Sickly! ... Nervous! ... Alas!

35 *Kaiser:* (*German*) Emperor.

Foppy-wops: see note to page 33 on *wops*. The addition of 'foppy' suggests that Mozart dislikes foreigners not just because they *are* foreign, but also because he is jealous of their elegant and cultivated manners (a 'fop' being a dandy). He prides himself on being straightforward and down-to-earth and Austrian to the core. See also note to page 17 on *Stanzerl ... Wolferl*.

36 *'forfeits':* game in which players have to pay a 'penalty' in return for failure to meet some requirement or condition demanded by the rules of play.

· 37 *Allez-oop!:* expression used by animal trainers or circus acrobats at the moment of bringing off a difficult feat.

38 *The Aurnhammer girl!:* Mozart was, in fact, the not altogether willing object of passionate advances from a number of young women. Josephine Aurnhammer, an accomplished pianist, was one such.

39 *can't get it up:* is incapable of achieving an erection.

Batti ... tesoro!: (*Italian*) Beat me, beat me, my treasure! This line is an interesting combination of the titles of two arias from Mozart's opera *Don Giovanni*, first produced on 29 October 1787. In Act 1, the peasant girl Zerlina sings 'Batti, batti' to her lover Masetto, in an effort to incite his anger – though, in fact, she succeeds in regaining his lost affection. In Act 2, the young hero Don Ottavio sings the love song 'Il mio tesoro' to Donna Anna, his beloved.

Madonna: name by which the Virgin Mary is addressed – literally 'my lady'.

40 *Caro Herr:* My dear sir (another combination of languages, this time Italian with German: see note to page 30 on *Enchanté, Fraulein*).

sorbetto: see note to page 15 on *sorbetti*.

41 *nod:* make mistakes.

Fantasia: kind of musical composition in which form is secondary to technical dexterity and showiness.

Trills: musical 'ornaments' adopted by both singers and instrumentalists – essentially a regular 'shake' developed on particular notes.

Aciaccatura: 'grace-note' played or sung very rapidly before another longer note; a type of ornamentation.

charlatans: frauds.

Clementi: Muzio (1752–1832) – Italian composer noted especially for his keyboard music. He eventually settled in England. See also note to page 22 on *I wish ... virtuoso*.

43 *'portfolio':* case or pair of boards for holding loose papers.

44 *delish:* short, colloquial form of 'delicious'.

Constanze ... stiff a name: 'Constanze' literally means 'one who is reliable, constant'.

La Generosa: (*Italian*) the generous woman.

La Statua: (*Italian*) the unbending, statuesque woman.

45 *Verona:* city of Northern Italy.

'*mouchoir*': handkerchief.

47 '*ferment*': turmoil, state of anguish.

Fiasco!: complete failure!

Nobile: (*Italian*) Honourable, noble.

48 '*Sinfonia Concertante*': concerto in three movements – see also note to page 12 on *concerto*.

49 '*the Kyrie from the C Minor Mass*': Mozart wrote a number of settings of the Mass during his lifetime, among the finest of which is the unfinished one in C Minor (first performed in August 1783). The Mass is divided into several movements, the first being the Kyrie Eleison ('Lord, have mercy upon us').

'*fortissimo*': very loudly.

'*counterpoint*': music in which two or more melodic lines are played or sung simultaneously.

'*continuum*': something which goes on unceasingly.

Capisco!: (*Italian*) I understand!

tanti: (*Italian*) very much.

50 *ancora:* (*Italian*) again.

God is not mocked: quotation from the Bible, *Epistle to the Galatians*, vi, 7: 'Be not deceived, God is not mocked; for whatsoever a man soweth, that shall he also reap'.

the spirit . . . listeth: also based on the Bible, *St John's Gospel*, iii, 8: 'The wind bloweth where it listeth, and thou hearest the sound thereof, but canst not tell whence it cometh, and whither it goeth'.

listeth: inclines, wishes.

Dio Ingiusto!: (*Italian*) Unfair, unjust God!

Nemico Eterno!: (*Italian*) Everlasting enemy!

51 *Amadeus:* the name means 'the beloved of God'.

Act Two

52 *cats . . . Rossini:* see note to page 7 on *Rossini*. One of Rossini's

most popular comic songs is a duet for two cats (sung by two sopranos) – hence Salieri's allusion.

Scarlatti: Giuseppe Domenico (1685–1757) – Italian composer, noted especially for his keyboard music, who spent much of his life in Spain.

stroll ... fugue: the story goes that the theme for one of Scarlatti's fugues (see also note to page 13) originated in the sounds made by a cat walking over the keys.

counterpoint: see note to page 49.

coloratura: high, elaborately ornamented passages of vocal music.

53 *soirée:* party or entertainment held of an evening.

Bach: Johann Sebastian (1685–1750) – German composer and one of the acknowledged great musicians of all time. Baron van Swieten is known to have been an enthusiastic admirer of Bach's music, some of which he commissioned Mozart to arrange for new combinations of instruments.

54 *'peignoir':* dressing-gown.

55 *Charmant!:* Charming! (But spoken in a tone of mild outrage.)

56 *A boy:* the Mozarts' first child, Raimond Leopold, had been born in mid-June 1783 but had survived barely two months. A second son, Karl Thomas – referred to here – was born on 21 September 1784. He died in 1856.

string quartets: pieces of music – generally in four movements – written for performance by a group of four stringed instruments: usually two violins, one viola and one 'cello.

Haydn: Franz Joseph (1732–1809) – celebrated and highly influential Austrian composer who was quick to appreciate Mozart's true genius.

'Rondo': the last movement of the concerto in question. Rondo form is one in which the principal musical subject or theme of a movement is repeated in alternation with other themes.

Semiramide: Salieri's opera was first performed in Munich in 1782.

57 *La Grotta di Trofonio:* 'The Grotto of Trofonio' was given its first performance in Vienna on 12 October 1785.

Danaius: Salieri's opera *Les Danaïdes* was first performed in Paris on 26 April 1784.

plaudits: applause.

58 *salons:* receptions, gatherings.

Princess Lichnowsky: wife of one of Mozart's aristocratic pupils, Prince Karl Lichnowsky.

Figaro! ... *Beaumarchais:* see note to page 27 on '*The Marriage of Figaro*'. Pierre Augustin Caron de Beaumarchais (1732–99) was a French playwright celebrated chiefly for his plays concerning the adventures of the valet-turned-barber, Figaro. Mozart was not the only composer to find Beaumarchais' plays suitable material for the operatic stage: see also note to page 7 on *Rossini*.

59 *boudoir:* lady's private room.

doodle: euphemism for 'penis'.

the ephemeral: that which does not last.

Hercules ... *Horatius:* celebrated heroic figures from classical legend.

60 *Mitridate* ... *Crete!:* titles of two of Mozart's earlier 'serious' operas on heroic themes. On the former, see note to page 12; on the latter, that to page 13.

quartet ... *quintet* ... *sextet:* types of vocal music written for four, five and six voices respectively.

61 *Buona fortuna:* (*Italian*) Good luck.

noddle: head.

62 *piccola:* (*Italian*) little.

Mi ... *atto?:* (*Italian*) I gather there's a ballet in the third act?

Si: (*Italian*) Yes.

E dimmi ... *opere?:* (*Italian*) And tell me – isn't it true that the Emperor has forbidden ballet in his operas?

Precisamente: (*Italian*) Exactly.

Oh, capisco! ... *ingegnoso!:* (*Italian*) Oh, I understand! How wonderful! Perfect! Really clever!

Pazienza: (*Italian*) Have patience.

64 *forte:* talent, strength.

65 *'flings':* walks in an angry manner.

Je prévois des merveilles!: (*French*) I can foresee wonders!

66 *'sotto voce':* in an undertone.

67 *Our religion ... them:* a slighting reference to the abundance of statues of saints in Italian churches.

69 *'Ah! Tutti contenti. Saremo così':* Ah! Everyone happy. Thus we shall be.

pasteboard: stiff board made of sheets of paper pasted together.

71 *crema al mascarpone:* see page 15.

I was ... boy: Mozart had been taken to England by his father in 1764, when he was eight years old.

72 *Fartsbishop:* until 1781, when he arrived in Vienna, Mozart had been employed as Court Composer to the Archbishop of Salzburg, Hieronymus Colloredo. But he had never seen eye to eye with his master and they had parted on bad terms: hence Mozart's disrespectful reference to him here.

Leopold Mozart is dead!: Leopold died in Salzburg on 28 May 1787.

73 *'tricorne':* three-cornered.

So rose ... Hell!: Mozart's opera, first seen in Prague on 29 October 1787, opens with a scene in which the dissolute Don Giovanni (better known to us, perhaps, as Don Juan) kills the father of the woman to whom he is making unwelcome advances. Towards the end of the opera, a statue of the murdered man comes to life and, in a moment of mocking bravado, Giovanni invites it to join him for supper. To his amazement, it appears at the appointed time and – as a punishment for his past sins – drags him to Hell.

'terzetto': piece of music for three voices.

Così Fan Tutte: Mozart's opera was first produced in Vienna on 26 January 1790: it concerns a plot by two young officers to test the love and faithfulness of their sweethearts, the sisters Fiordiligi and Dorabella. 'Soave sia il vento' is a song of farewell for the two men as they take ship, supposedly for foreign parts, the singers wishing that they may be blessed with a kindly breeze. The musical quotation is doubly appropriate, placed as it is just after Salieri's reference to his own efforts being 'calmed in convention'.

74 *Chamber Composer:* the office to which Mozart succeeded in December 1787 (not 1790 as the sequence of events and references in the play suggests) was actually that of Royal and Imperial Court Composer.

florin: gold coin, current throughout Europe, so called because it was first struck in the Italian city of Florence.

75 *Vous nous faites honneur!: (French)* You are doing us a great honour!

Contredanzes: wide variety of dances supposed to be of country origin.

76 *Kapellmeister Bonno is dead!:* Bonno died in 1788.

Evviva: (Italian) Long live.

77 *'The Prater':* see note to page 2.

'palpably': plainly, obviously.

78 *Rauhensteingasse:* street in a poor quarter of Vienna.

79 *'Masonic symbols . . . ritual apron':* the order of Freemasons (see note to page 13) originally developed among the craftsmen who built the great European cathedrals during the Middle Ages. Hence, many of the symbols associated with masonry have to do with building and architectural design (dividers, hammer, chisel and so on) and the craftsman's apron is part of the ritual attire worn at masonic ceremonies.

fugues of Bach: see note to page 53 on *Bach.*

Schikaneder: Emanuel Johann (1751–1812) – Austrian writer and theatre director.

theatre in the suburbs: situated in the Viennese suburb of Wieden.

80 *vaudeville:* play with incidental (usually comic) songs and dances.

'Monostatos . . . "Das Klinget so herrlich, Das Klinget so schön!"': Mozart's opera *Die Zauberflöte* received its first

performance on 30 September 1791. It has a strange, fairy-tale plot in which one of the central figures is the priest of Isis, Sarastro. At one point in Act I, Sarastro's Moorish servant, Monostatos, is – together with a group of slaves – put into a trance by the sound of some magic bells. The song tells of their wonderment at the magical beauty of the sound.

81 *glockenspiel:* percussion instrument which gives a delicate, bell-like sound. It consists of a keyboard of metal plates which are struck by two small hammers held by the player.

82 *contredanze:* see note to page 75.

Non più andrai ... girando!: There'll be an end to your amorous flitting about by day and night!

See also note to page 27 on *'The Marriage of Figaro'*. The warning has now been transferred, in Constanze's half-crazed singing, to Mozart himself.

84 *Poppy ... pappa-pappa!:* the game Mozart and Constanze play is strongly reminiscent of the duet in Act II of *Die Zauberflöte* in which two of the characters, Papageno and Papagena, are finally united.

a boy: Franz Xavier Wolfgang Mozart was born on 26 July 1791. He died in 1844. After the birth of Karl Thomas in 1784, Constanze had given birth to three other children, none of whom survived more than a few months.

85 *Baden: not* the celebrated German spa, but a small town 16 miles (26 kilometres) south of Vienna, noted for its mineral springs.

Requiem Mass: mass for the repose of the souls of the dead.

87 *tenement:* apartment building.

'blowsy and bedizened': fat cheeked and gaudily dressed.

pungent: foul smelling.

'"Heil sei euch Geweihten"': – celebrates the final victory of beauty and wisdom after a series of ordeals in the course of the opera.

88 *I saw his father ... Highest Priest of the Order:* see also note to page 80 on *'Monostatos ... "Das Klinget so herrlich, Das Klinget so schön!"'*. Whereas the father-figure in *Don Giovanni* is

vengeful and threatening (see note to page 73 on *So rose . . . Hell!*), that of Sarastro in *Die Zauberflöte* is benign and forgiving.

There . . . beside me!: the *zauberflöte* of Mozart's opera is a flute with magical powers. Salieri sees Mozart as being himself the magic flute through whose notes God speaks to and enchants mankind.

89 *vulgarian*: vulgar, common person.

91 *the words . . . venite a cena!*: see also note to page 73 on *So rose . . . Hell!*. The Italian means 'Oh most noble statue, come to dinner!'

92 *It's not finished!*: Mozart refers, of course, to the Requiem Mass – see page 85.

Kyrie . . . Eleison: see note to page 49 on '*the Kyrie from the C Minor Mass*'.

double fugue: fugue with two subjects or main themes.

clavier: term used in Germany to denote any kind of keyboard instrument – fortepiano, harpsichord, piano and so on.

93 '*elevates . . . Communion Service*': in the course of the Mass or service of Holy Communion, the priest offers the bread or wafer to God by raising it over the altar and then kneeling.

Eccomi: (*Italian*) Here I am.

94 *Oragna . . . fa!*: a childish nonsense rhyme.

'*treble*': the high-pitched voice of a young boy.

96 '*Lacrimosa*': the seventh movement of Mozart's Requiem. He did not live to write more than the first eight bars of the movement, which – like much of the rest of the work – was left to be completed by his pupil Süssmayr.

goose: colloquial term for a foolish person.

97 *kidney failure*: see note to page 4 on *Syphilis*.

lime pit: grave in which a body is buried without a coffin and in which decomposition is accelerated by the presence of quicklime (calcium oxide).

'*assiduously*': diligently, carefully.

a Danish diplomat: Georg Nikolaus von Nissen, who was a

devoted admirer of Mozart and later wrote the composer's biography.

98 *schilling:* unit of Austrian currency.

salvoes of cannon ... Battle Symphony: Beethoven (see note to page 2) wrote his so-called Battle Symphony to commemorate Wellington's victory at the Battle of Victoria (Spain). It was given its first performance in Vienna in 1813 at a concert for the benefit of Austrian soldiers wounded in the battle. It contains quotations from patriotic British pieces such as 'Rule, Britannia' and 'God Save the King', as well as loud passages of imitation cannon fire.

99 *Waterloo:* Wellington's famous victory over Napoleon at the Battle of Waterloo (Belgium) took place in 1815.

Nemico ... implacabile!: Enemy of Enemies! Merciless God!

101 *Beethoven's Conversation Book:* see note to page 2 on *Beethoven*. Because, in his deafness, Beethoven was unable to hold normal conversations, his visitors wrote what they would otherwise have spoken aloud in a notebook for him to read.

'gargoyle': grotesquely carved water spout, common on the roofs of old churches.

German Musical Times: newspaper devoted to music criticism and articles about the musical world.

102 *'Benediction':* blessing.

'Masonic Funeral Music': Mozart's solemn *Mauerische Trauermusik*, for strings and wind instruments, was written to mark the deaths, in 1785, of two of his brother masons.

(*Acknowledgements:* I am indebted to Jacqueline Worswick and Robin Nelson for their help over some of the Italian and musical references in these Notes – Richard Adams.)

Further reading

Amadeus

If you are interested in investigating the differences between version 3 of *Amadeus* and its predecessors, version 1 is available in this country from André Deutsch (hardback) and version 2 from Penguin (paperback).

A new translation of Pushkin's verse drama *Mozart and Salieri*, prepared by Anthony Wood, is published by Angel Books (1982).

Useful background material on Mozart's life can be found in Erich Valentin's *Mozart and his World* (Thames and Hudson, 1959), while the definitive study of the composer remains Alfred Einstein's *Mozart: his character, his work* (Cassell, 1946).

Other plays by Peter Shaffer

Paperback editions of most of Shaffer's plays are readily available. Penguin's *Three Plays* (1976) contains *Equus*, *Shrivings* and *Five Finger Exercise*; while *Four Plays* (1981 – also Penguin) brings together *The Private Ear*, *The Public Eye*, *White Liars* and *Black Comedy*.

The Longman Study Texts series includes editions of *The Royal Hunt of the Sun* (with introduction and notes by Peter Cairns) and *Equus* (with introduction and notes by T. S. Pearce).

Study questions

1 To what extent can any work of art be said to have an independent life of its own?

2 How important is our awareness of the artist's original intentions in our proper appreciation of his or her work?

3 Give a carefully prepared (a) reading (b) performance of the opening scene of *Amadeus*, paying particular attention to the musical effects it contains.

4 Compare and contrast the speeches Shaffer gives to Salieri and Mozart in this play.

5 What does the rejection of Mozart by the cultivated society of his own day suggest about the nature of the relationships between genius and society in any age?

6 How would you distinguish between historical truth and dramatic truth? Illustrate your answer with examples from *Amadeus*.

7 What issues does *Amadeus* seem to you to be concerned with?

8 Do you agree that 'goodness is nothing in the furnace of art', that moral considerations have no place in the workings of creativity?

9 For whom, in the end, do you feel the greater sympathy, Mozart or Salieri?

10 Write about the different types of irony in *Amadeus*.

11 Show, with examples, the variety of humour Shaffer employs in *Amadeus*.

12 Do you agree that *Amadeus* both delights and provokes us to thought?